Study Guide

for

Schmalleger and Bartollas

Juvenile Delinquency

prepared by

Tom McAninch
Scott Community College

PEARSON

Boston   New York   San Francisco
Mexico City   Montreal   Toronto   London   Madrid   Munich   Paris
Hong Kong   Singapore   Tokyo   Cape Town   Sydney

ISBN-13: 978-0-205-52038-1
ISBN-10:   0-205-52038-3

Printed in the United States of America

10 9 8 7 6 5 4 3 2 1   11 10 09 08 07

TABLE OF CONTENTS

Chapter 5. Social Process Theories

Chapter 6. Social Interactionist Theories of Delinquency

Chapter 7. Gender and Delinquency

Chapter 8. The Family and Delinquency

Chapter 9. The School and Delinquency

Chapter 10. Gangs and Delinquency

Chapter 11. Drugs and Delinquency

Chapter 12. Prevention, Diversion, and Treatment

Chapter 13. The Juvenile Justice Process

Chapter 14. The Police and the Juvenile

Chapter 15. The Juvenile Court

Chapter 16. Juvenile Corrections

CHAPTER 1: ADOLESCENCE AND DELINQUENCY

Learning Objectives

After reading this chapter you should be able to answer the following questions:

1. What does it mean to be an adolescent in American Society today?

2. Are adolescents treated the same now as in the past?

3. What are the problem behaviors that characterize adolescence?

4. How can delinquency be defined?

5. What is a status offense?

6. How have delinquents been handled throughout history?

7. What are the major themes of this text?

CHAPTER SUMMARY

This chapter places delinquent behavior within the wider context of adolescent problem behaviors. Adolescents most likely to become delinquent are high-risk youths who are involved in multiple problem behaviors. Problem behaviors include school failure and dropout, teenage pregnancy and fatherhood, drug use, and delinquency. About one in every four adolescents is at high risk of engaging in multiple problem behaviors.

Bartollas uses a social focus to help understand juvenile delinquency in America. The history of dealing with juvenile misbehavior in the United States has been one of taking authority away from the family and at the same time becoming increasingly dissatisfied with the state's means of handling juvenile crime.

Parens patriae is the legal context and philosophy for dealing with juvenile delinquency, through which the juvenile court becomes a substitute parent for wayward children. The task of juvenile court is to reconcile the best interest of the child with the protection of society. Additionally, juveniles are arrested for *status offenses*, which would not be defined as criminal if adults committed them.

Delinquency in the United States occurs in a social context that has become more and more child oriented. Lower-class youth are often viewed differently by the juvenile system and receive more punitive sanctions. Conversely, middle-and upper-class youth traditionally receive less restrictive sanctions.

However, there is increased concern that society needs to "get tough" on juvenile crime. The present focus is on serious and repeat juvenile offenders. Both the public and its policymakers attempt to hold juvenile offenders accountable for violent crimes through tough sanctions.

Bartollas purports a major goal of this text is to reduce the social cost of letting vast numbers of young people grow up without realizing their potential. Equally, Bartollas proposes the means by with youngsters in our society can realize their potential and lead productive and satisfying lives.

LECTURE OUTLINE

I. **Introduction**
   - The legacy of the Seniors of Winslow Township High School
   - A term used to define the life interval between childhood and adulthood.
   - Lengthening of adolescence in U.S. culture increases crisis and struggles.
   - Unmet childhood needs fester into socially unacceptable behaviors.

II. **The Changing Treatment of Adolescents**
   - The end of child labor (1914) was a watershed in the development of modern adolescence.
   - Compulsory education laws held that adolescents needed guidance and control.
   - Legal protections in the 1960s and 1970s highlighted special attention and support.
   - Erickson suggested childhood repression due to lack of young people's rights.
   - Influence of economic, social and political forces.

III. **Youth at Risk**
   - Nanette J. Davis suggests *"structural arrangements"* of racial discrimination, poverty, violence, and drugs/alcohol leads to invisible youth crisis. American institutions contribute to crisis.
   - Warehousing approach for juvenile delinquents.

   A. **High-Risk Behaviors**
      - High-risk youths experience multiple difficulties such as economically stressed families, physical/sexual abuse, educational/vocational deficits, and drug/alcohol abuse.
      - Gottfredson and Hirschi suggest lack of self-control as a common factor for high-risk behavior.
      - One in four adolescence is at high risk of engaging in multiple problem behaviors.
      - Delinquency is a legal term from Illinois 1899 law.
      - Juveniles are five times more likely to be arrested for property crimes than violent crimes.
      - *Status offenses* are acts related to age, meaning they would not be defined criminal if committed by adults.
      - Three times as many youths are arrested for committing status offenses as violent crime.

IV. **Juvenile Court Codes and Definitions of delinquency**
   - Rehabilitative laws based on the philosophy of *Parens Patriae* were enacted to eliminate arbitrary treatment of juveniles.
   - Court has jurisdiction in delinquency, dependency, and neglect cases.
   - Diverse definitions of delinquency have developed.
   - Controversy surrounds the issue of how long juveniles should remain under control of the court.

V. What is a Status Offense?
- Various definitions of delinquency in juvenile codes (see Box 1.2)
- Delinquency in America: Rise in Income Improves Children's Behavior

A. Explanations For Status Offense Behavior
- Many come from single-parent homes.
- Parents view status offenders as defiant, demanding, and obnoxious, leading to struggles.
- Status offenders often are hyperactive and treated with Ritalin.
- Chesney-Lind suggests a double standard for female status offenders.

B. Offense Behavior of Status Offenders and Delinquents
- Charles W. Thomas contends status offender's progress to delinquent offenses.
- National study of status offenders identified three groups: "heavies", "lightweights" and "conforming youths." This study disputes a linkage between status and delinquent offenses.
- In sum, status offenders are *not* likely to escalate to more serious behaviors.

C. Social Control and the Status Offender
- Confining of status offenders comes under attack in the 1970s. Offenders stayed longer in training schools than delinquents and institutionalization became destructive.
- 1974 Juvenile Justice and Delinquency Act was an impetus for *deinstitutionalization*.
- *Deinstitutionalization of Status Offenders Project (DSO)* revealed little change in the processing of status offenders. In fact, detention of African-American status offenders increased.
- Redefining status offenders as "delinquent" allows for *invisible institutionalization*.
- Some states have decriminalized status offenses.

VI. The Handling of Juvenile Delinquents

A. The Colonial Period (1636-1823)
- Family is the primary source for social control of children. Young chronic offenders were disciplined in public view, such as whippings, dunkings, the stocks and expulsion from the community.

B. The Houses of Refuge Period (1824-1898)
- Disillusioned with family, *houses of refuge* were proposed. Intended to protect children from weak and criminal parents.
- Discipline was firm and harsh. Family authority is superseded by that of the State.

C. The Juvenile Court Period (1899-1966)
- First juvenile court in Cook County, Illinois 1899 is based on the legal concept of *parens patriae*.
- Wayward children were considered "wards of the state" and less responsible for their actions.
- Poverty, ills of city life, inadequate families, schools, and neighborhoods are contributing factors.

D. The Juvenile Rights Period (1967-1975)
- The courts are accused of capricious and arbitrary justice. Supreme Court hands down several landmark cases to ensure children will have *due process*.
- Community based programs receive enthusiastic responses. Some believed training schools would eventually be phased out.

E. The Reform Agenda of the Late 1970s
- The major purpose is to divert status offenses from a criminal to a noncriminal setting.
- Discourage the practice of jailing juveniles and encouraged community-based services.
- Liberal blunder of failing to pay attention to serious juvenile crime became an Achilles' heel.

F. Social Control and Juvenile Crime in the 1980s
- Public demands for something to be done about serious juvenile crime.
- 1984 National Advisory Committee for *Juvenile Justice and Delinquency Prevention* (NAC) leads to a focus on serious, violent, and chronic offenders. Rejects deinstitutionalization.
- Teen pregnancies, drug/alcohol abuse, and teen suicides fueled a time of *"getting tough."*
- Growing acceptance of parents needing to be stricter with their children.
- Reagan administration encourages five trends: (1) preventative detention; (2) transfer violent juveniles to adult court; (3) mandatory/determinate sentencing; (4) increased confinement; and (5) enforcement of the death penalty.

G. Contemporary Delinquency and U.S. Society
- The "crack epidemic" becomes a major impetus for the spread of drug trafficking street gangs.
- Use of guns and drugs contribute to increased murder rates among young people.
- States pass legislation leading to nine initiatives in juvenile justice: (1) curfews; (2) parental responsibility laws; (3) combating street gangs; (4) the movement toward graduated sanctions; (5) juvenile boot camps; (6) youth and guns; (7) juvenile proceedings; (8) juvenile transfer to criminal courts, and (9) expanded sentencing authority.

VII. Themes in the Study of Delinquency

A. Focus on Social Context
- Historical context influences current perceptions.
- Legal context establishes the definition of delinquent behavior.
- Sociocultural context examines the relationship between social institutions and delinquency.
- Economic context examines conditions and factors in which delinquents live.
- Political context shapes local and national policy decisions on youth crime.
- A contextual analysis reminds students of delinquency that a variety of forces on several levels affect youth crime.

B. Delinquency International
- Young killers at heart of capital punishment fight in Japan

C. Delinquency Across the Life Course
- Glen H. Elder Jr. identified four key factors that determine life course: 1) location in time and place, 2) linked lives, 3) human agency, and 4) timing of lives.
- All levels of social action interact and mutually influence each other as a result of contact with other individuals sharing similar experiences.

D. Policy Oriented Analysis
- Designing of recommendations that provide helpful directions for dealing effectively with adolescents in general and particularly those rendered delinquent.

Adolescence: The life interval between childhood and adulthood, usually the period between the ages of twelve and eighteen years.

Deinstitutionalization of Status Offender Project (DSO): A project that evaluated the effects of deinstitutionalization of status offenders in eight states and prompter a national evaluation.

Houses of Refuge: Institutions that were designed by eighteenth-a and nineteenth-century reformers to provide an orderly disciplined environment similar to that of the "ideal" Puritan family.

Human Agency: The active role juveniles take in their lives; the fact that juveniles are not merely subject to social and structural constraints but make choices and decisions based on the alternatives that they see before them.

Juvenile: A youth at or below the upper age of juvenile court jurisdiction in a particular state.

Juvenile Delinquency: An act committed by a minor that violates the penal code of the government with authority over the area in which the act occurs.

Juvenile Justice and Delinquency Prevention Act of 1974: A federal law that established a juvenile justice office within the Law Enforcement Assistance Administration to provide funds for the prevention and control of youth crime.

Life Course Perspective: A sociological framework suggesting that four key factors determine the shape of the life course: location in time and place, linked lives, human agency, and timing of lives.

Parens Patriae: A Medieval English doctrine that sanctioned the right of the Crown to intervene in natural family relations whenever a child's welfare was threatened. The philosophy of the juvenile court is based on this legal concept.

Status Offender: A juvenile who commits a minor act that is considered illegal only because he or she is underrate. Various terms used to refer to status offenders in clued MINS (minors I need of supervision), CHINS (children in need of supervision), CHINA (children in need of assistance), PINS (persons in need of supervision), FINS (families in need of supervision), and JINS (juveniles in need of supervision).

Status Offense: A nondelinquent/noncriminal offense; an offense that is illegal for underage persons, but not for adults. Status offenses include curfew violations, incorrigibility, running away, truancy, and underage drinking.

Multiple Choice:

1. Each chapter begins with a particular vignette to introduce the issues in the chapter. This chapter starts with a story about _____.
   a. The World Trade Center
   b. Winslow Township High School
   c. The Vice Lords
   d. Guns in schools in the south
   e. Assaults of young women by football players

2. The Chicago Area Projects are associated with _____.
   a. James Q. Wilson and O.W. Wilson
   b. Richard Cloward and Lloyd Ohlin
   c. Frank Schmalleger and Thomas McAninch
   d. Edwin Sutherland and Donald Cressey
   e. Clifford Shaw and Henry McKay

3. The life interval between childhood and adulthood, usually the period between the ages of twelve and eighteen years.
   a. Cohort
   b. Peer group
   c. Adolescence
   d. "The Crazy Years"
   e. Juvenile

4. Delinquency _____ during the adolescent years for several reasons.
   a. decreases
   b. increases
   c. remains consistent
   d. peaks in the preteens and then declines during adolescence

5. Lloyd de Mause is know for his work in _____.
   a. teenage serial killers
   b. American gang development
   c. juvenile institutions
   d. runaway children
   e. Psychohistory

6. The proportion of children who are Hispanic was 9 % of the population in 1980. Today the proportion of the children who are Hispanic is _____.
a. 7%
b. 9%
c. 12%
d. 15%
e. 19%

7. During the Clinton administration, from 1992 to 2000, there were almost _____.
a. four million new children added to the welfare roles
b. four million children lifted out of poverty
c. juvenile crime increased 20%
d. juvenile crime

8. The Children's Defense Fund's publication, *State of American Children, 2005* refers to the American juvenile justice system as an (a) _____.
a. example for all the world to immolate
b. complete and total mess
c. cradle to prison pipeline
d. system which has great promise if it was 100% funded
e. a system that offers help to those children that re seeking it

9. Juvenile delinquency is defined as _____.
a. a behavior committed by a minor which is unsocial and in violation of societies' norms
b. sociopathic behavior by a juvenile
c. an act committed by a minor that violates the penal code of the government with authority over the area in which the act occurs.
d. an act such as truancy, running away from home or disobeying parents
e. an act that would not be criminal if an adult committed it but is criminal when a juvenile commits it

10. An example of a crime that a juvenile can be arrested for but an adult cannot be arrest for is _____.
a. truancy
b. incorrigibility
c. curfew violations
d. runaway behavior
e. all of the above

11. The *In re Poff* decision dealt with the issue of _____.
a. search and seizure of a juvenile
b. questioning of a juvenile
c. detainment of a juvenile
d. the general rights of a juvenile, protections afforded by the Juvenile Court

12. Children in need of protection and services are know as _____.
a. CHINA
b. CHINS
c. CHIPS
d. MINS
e. JINS

13. Children in need of assistance are known as _____.
a. CHINA
b. CHINS
c. CHIPS
d. MINS
e. JINS

14. Families in need of supervision are know as _____.
a. CHINA
b. CHINS
c. CHIPS
d. MINS
e. FINS

15. The Journal of the American Medical Association noted that as incomes of families with children increase deviant behaviors _____.
a. increased at the same rate
b. increased at a much higher rate
c. decreased
d. remained the same, there was no relationship between income and deviance

16. Most states sit the upper age limit for the juvenile court at _____.
a. 14
b. 15
c. 16
d. 17
e. 18

17. Who believes that status offenders are very similar in offense behavior with delinquent offenders and tend to progress from status to delinquent offenses.
a. James Q. Wilson and O.W. Wilson
b. Richard Cloward and Lloyd Ohlin
c. W. I. Thomas
d. John Peterson
e. Clifford Shaw and Henry McKay

18. Solomon Kobrin, Frank R. Hellum, and John W. Peterson identified three groups of status offenders. One of the following is not one of those types.
a. the new boys
b. the heavies
c. the lightweights
d. the conforming youths

19. The history of juvenile justice in the United States actually began in the _____.
a. colonial period
b. during the house of refuge   (1824-1898
c. when the first juvenile court was formed in 1899
d. at the start of WWI in 1917

20. Institutions that were designed by eighteenth and nineteenth century reformers to provide an orderly disciplined environment similar to that of the "ideal" Puritan family were called _____.
a. Homes for children
b. Family Safe Houses
c. Houses of refuge
d. Children's Homes
e. Juvenile Institutions

21. A Medieval English doctrine that sanctioned the right of the Crown to intervene in natural family relations whenever a child's welfare was threatened. The philosophy of the juvenile court is based on this legal concept.
a. *parens patriae*
b. The Power of the King
c. The Divine Right of Kings
d. in loco parentis
e. none of the above

22. The first juvenile court was created in _____.
a. New York City
b. Boston
c. Chicago (Cook County)
d. Denver
e. Los Angeles

23. The life interval between childhood and adulthood, usually the period between the ages of twelve and eighteen years is called _____.
a. adolescence
b. childhood
c. the crazy years
d. the between years
e. pre-adult years

24. The major thrust of the Reagan administration's crime control policies for juveniles was _____.
a. to build more treatment centers
b. to improve education in America
c. to get tough on crime
d. to get more counseling for the troubled youth who need it
e. all of the above

25. The constitutionality of curfews has been litigated in several states. What is the current position of the court.
a. curfews are unconstitutional because it is discrimination based on age.
b. curfews are unconstitutional because they are arbitrary, each state sets different standards
c. curfews are constitutional and should be left up to the states
d. curfews are constitutional IF they all have the same rules

True/False

1) The concept of childhood, as reflected in today's child-centered culture, is a relatively recent phenomenon.

2) Delinquency decreases during the time of adolescence.

3) African American children are more likely to be sick because they are poor.

4) Two out of five African America babies today are born into poverty and face a losing struggle with poverty throughout childhood.

5) The population of children in the United States is becoming larger and is growing more racially and ethnically diverse.

6. Juveniles are arrest for committing more violent crime than property crime.

7. Adults can be arrest for status offenses in the same manor as a juvenile.

8. A burglary is an example of a status offense.

9. J. G. Weis and associates found that juveniles who began their offender careers engaging in status offenses only were not likely to graduate into more serious crime.

10. The history of juvenile justice in the United State actually began in the colonial period.

11. A Medieval English doctrine that sanctioned the right of the Crown to intervene in natural family relations whenever a child's welfare was threatened. The philosophy of the juvenile court is based on this legal concept and is called in loco parentis

12. The U.S. Supreme Court has declared juvenile curfews unconstitutional because it is discrimination based on age.

Fill-in-the-blank:

1. The life interval between childhood and adulthood; usually the period between the ages of twelve and eighteen years is called _____.

2. A project that evaluates the effects of deinstitutionalization of status offenders in eight states and prompted a national evaluation is called the _____.

3. Institutions that were designed by eighteenth and nineteenth century reformers to provide an orderly disciplined environment similar to the "ideal" Puritan family is called

_____.

4. An act committed by a minor that violates the penal code of the government with the authority over the area in which the act occurs is called _____.

5. A federal law that established a juvenile justice office within the Law Enforcement Assistance Administration to provide funds for the prevention and control of youth crime was called the

_____.

6. A sociological framework suggesting that four key factors determine the shape of the life course: location in time and place, linked lives, human agency, and timing of lives is called the

_____.

7. A Medieval English doctrine that sanctioned the right of the Crown to intervene in natural family relations whenever a child's welfare was threatened was called _____. The philosophy of the juvenile court is based on this legal concept.

8. A juvenile who commits a minor act that is considered illegal only because he or she is underage is called a _____.

9. Offenses like curfew violations, incorrigibility, running away, truancy, and underage drinking are called _____.

Essay Questions

1. According to the *State of American Children 2005*, how does poverty affect children?

2. Children are know as MINS, CHINS, JINS, CHINA, PINS, CHIPS, and FINS. What do all these acronyms state for?

3. According to the News Box, Delinquency in America, what is the affect of income on delinquency?

4. The juvenile court's jurisdiction over status offenders is a highly volatile issues. What are the pros and cons for having the juvenile court involved with status offenders?

5. The major thrust of the Reagan administration's crime control policies for juvenile were to get tough on serious and violent juvenile crime. This idea encouraged five trends in the juvenile justice system. Briefly state each of those five trends.

Answers Practice Test

Multiple Choice:

1. Answer: b   2. Answer: e   3. Answer: c   4. Answer: b   5. Answer: e   6. Answer: e
7. Answer: b   8. Answer: c   9. Answer: c   10. Answer: e   11. Answer: d   12. Answer: c
13. Answer: a   14. Answer: e   15. Answer: c   16. Answer: d   17. Answer: c
18. Answer: a   19. Answer: a   20. Answer: c   21. Answer: a   22. Answer: c
23. Answer: a   24. Answer: c   25. Answer: c

True/False:

1. True   2. False   3. True   4. True   5. True   6. False   7. False   8. False   9. True
10. True   11. False   12. False

Fill-in-the-blank:

1. Adolescence
2. Deinstitutionalization of Status Offenders Project (DSO)
3. Houses of refuge
4. Juvenile delinquency
5. Juvenile Justice and Delinquency Prevention Act of 1974
6. Life course perspective
7. Parens patriae
8. Status offender
9. Status offense

WEBSITES

Visit the Office of Juvenile Justice and Delinquency Prevention (OJJDP) Web site via www. justicestudies.com/WebPlaces

Visit the Youth Risk Behavior Surveillance System (YRBSS) Web site, part of the Centers for Disease Control and Prevention, via www.justicestudeies.com/ WebPlaces

Visit the Child Trends databank, with the latest national trends and research on over 100 key indicators of child and youth well-being, via www.justicestudies.com/WebPlaces.

Visit the U.S. department of health and Human Services (HHS) Child Welfare Information gateway via justicestudies.com/WebPlaces

View the OJJDP PowerPoint presentation " Juvenile Population Characteristics," at justicestudies.com/WebPlaces

www.barefootsworld.net/parensp.html

www.ncjrs.org

CHAPTER 2: THE MEASUREMENT AND NATURE OF DELINQUENCY

LEARNING OBJECTIVES

After reading this chapter you should be able to answer the following questions:

1. What do official and unofficial statistics tell us about the extent of juvenile delinquency?

2. Is juvenile violent crime increasing in the United States?

3. How do such social factors as gender, racial and ethnic backgrounds, and social class relate to juvenile delinquency?

4. What other dimensions of offending appear to be important in delinquent behavior?

5. Why do the majority of juvenile offenders exit from delinquent activity by the end of their adolescent years?

CHAPTER SUMMARY

This chapter discusses the various official and unofficial methods used to measure juvenile delinquency. Official methods of measure include *Uniform Crime Reports, Juvenile Court Statistics, self-report and victimization studies (NCVS)*. All of which have contributed to a number of important findings about youth crime in the United States. Measurement methods are commonly affected by *validity* and *reliability* problems.

The various forms of statistics on juvenile delinquency have far more agreement than disagreement and seek to answer pressing questions about juvenile delinquency. The studies have suggested that rates of delinquency in the United States have either leveled off or are declining. Homicide rates have declined rather dramatically since 1993 and the resurgence of a violent crime wave is unlikely to materialize in the near future. There is little evidence to support that there are more juvenile "monsters" than in the past. However, gang members and other serious offenders continue to commit brutal crimes.

Research indicates juveniles commit a disproportionate number of property and violent offenses, carry more guns than in the past, and youth crime is primarily focused in the lower-class youths. Additionally, males commit more delinquent acts than females, nonwhites more frequent and serious acts than whites, and urban youths commit more serious acts than rural youths do.

Intervention strategies by the juvenile justice system frequently make behaviors worse rather than better. Some evidence exits that youthful offenders progress to increasingly serious forms of delinquent behaviors. Youths who begin offending early tend to have long delinquent careers.

Delinquents generally show a great deal of versatility, rather than specialization, in committing offenses.

Life Course criminology is concerned with explaining individual changes in offending throughout life. *Desistance*, or terminating delinquent behavior, is strongly related to the maturation process. In the midst of the continuity of childhood antisocial behavior, some adults experience *turning points*, or change, usually related to such matters as stable jobs, or a satisfying marriage or family life.

LECTURE OUTLINE

I. Introduction
- *Prevalence of delinquency* related to proportion of cohort and specific age.
- *Incidence of delinquency* refers to the frequency of offending or number of events.
- Murder by an 11 year old child.

II. Measuring Delinquency
- 1870 Congress created Department of Justice for federal record keeping.
- Creation of *Uniform Crime Reports* and the FBI to serve as clearinghouse for data.
- UCR's only measure reported crime, not hidden delinquency.
- Problems of UCR's include underestimating crime and police manipulation.
- Amnesty Program Takes Ai at UK's "knife Culture"

A. Crime by Age Groups
- Juveniles ages ten to seventeen are 29.8 percent of all arrests in U.S.
- Juveniles account for 33 percent of all burglary arrests, 25 percent of all robbery arrests, 24 percent of weapon arrests, 14 percent of aggravated assault and 9 percent of murder arrests.
- Between 1993 and 2003 juvenile arrests for murder declined about one-fourth.
- Juveniles were 13.8 percent of all drug arrests in 2002.
- Nonwhites are arrested in higher proportions for violent crimes than whites. Amnesty Program takes Aim at UK's "Knife Culture".

B. Youth Crime Trends
- Per UCR's Part I juvenile arrests declined from 45 percent to 27.5 percent between 1971 and 2005. Property crimes declined from 51 percent to 32 percent
- Alfred Blumstein predicts more guns will lead to crime wave in ten to fifteen years.
- James Alan Fox predicts juvenile violence will increase by 2005.
- Reduction in violent crime related to more effective gun policies, increased incarceration, more effective policing, more services, and maturation of crime-prone age groups.

III. Juvenile Court Statistics
- Inaugurated in 1926 by Children's Bureau of the Department of Labor for the general nature and extent of problems brought before the juvenile court.

- Statistical problems include time lag, small percentage of total offenses, and represent only an estimate of actual crimes before the court.
- Drug offenses showed a dramatic increase between 1987 and 1999.

IV. Cohort Studies
- *Cohort* is a group who has something in common such as age, high school, arrest dates and are studied over time.
- Findings indicate that most serious offenses are committed by lower-class minority males.
- Punishment by the system tends to encourage future criminality.
- Males commit more serious offenses than females.

V. Self-Reports and Official Statistics Compared

A. Reliability and Validity of Self Report Studies
- *Validity* is questionable in self-report studies
- *Reliability* refers to consistency of a questionnaire or interview responses.

B. Findings of Self-Report Studies
- Porterfield's first study of hidden delinquency concluded delinquency is widespread and that no relationship exists between social class and delinquency.
- Recent self-report studies suggest a large portion of juveniles commit violent acts.
- The Denver study suggests a smaller percentage of serious delinquents are using harder drugs.
- The Pittsburgh study reports that African-American boys committed more serious acts of delinquency than white boys (51 percent compared to 28 percent).
- The Rochester study reports levels of attachment and involvement are related to delinquency.

C. Youth Crime Trends
- Illicit drug use peaked around 1979 and declined into the 1990s.
- Marijuana use increases from 1992-1996.

VI. Victimization Surveys
- Began in 1972 in conjunction with the Census Bureau.
- Respondents are asked about perception of crime, extent of fear, and attitudes about crime.
- Limitations include no information on status offenses, victimless crimes, and inaccurate accounts.
- Per the NCVS violent crime fell 54 percent and property crime declined 50 percent between 1993 and 2002.
- African-American males more likely than whites to be victims of violent crime.
- Being victimized increases ones likelihood of offending.
- Victimization findings include more crime is committed than reported. Where one lives will increase/decrease the probability of being victimized. Theft crimes of less than $250 is the most frequently committed crime. Juveniles are more likely to commit crimes than other age groups. African-Americans and females are more likely to report crime.

VII. Social Factors related to Delinquency

A. Gender and Delinquent Behavior
- According to the Per UCR males are arrested more than females.
- Males are likely to be arrested for stolen property, vandalism, weapon offenses, and assaults. Seven times more likely for drug offenses and five times more likely for violent offenses than females.
- Females are likely to be arrested for running away, and prostitution.
- Gender, race, and class create a *"multiple marginality"* per Meda Chesney-Lind.

B. Racial/Ethnic Background and Delinquent Behavior
- African-Americans are arrested more frequently than whites, however self-report measures indicate little difference in involvement exists between African-Americans and whites, per two national studies.
- African-American females are more likely than white females to be victimized by violent crime.

C. Social Class and Delinquency
- Studies suggest that upper-and middle-class juveniles are as delinquent as their lower-class peers.
- Hirschi's survey states that little association exits between income, education, and occupation with delinquency.
- The data provides no firm evidence that social class is a salient factor in delinquency.

VIII. Dimensions of Delinquent Behavior

A. Age of Onset
- Early–onset delinquents tend to persist in offending behavior and are more likely to be arrested.
  The Social World of the delinquent

B. Escalation of Offenses
- Mixed findings reveal that early intervention by the juvenile system may lead to increased delinquency.
- Farrington contends males peak at age seventeen for nonviolent crimes and eighteen for violent crimes.
- Loeber suggests developmental interconnected pathways lead to a delinquent career.

C. Specialization of Offenses
- Most specialized offenses include running away, burglary, motor vehicle theft, drinking liquor, incorrigibility, violating curfew, truancy, and using drugs.
- *Specialization* tends to increase with successive number of referrals.
- Females tend to specialize in running away (status offenses) more than males.
- Recent data suggests early life course offenders are more versatile in their offending than those who begin offending at a later age.

D. Chronic Offending
- *Chronic offenders* constitute the majority of active offenders.
- Chronic offenders are more involved in violent crime and come from ever-growing minority underclass that finds itself trapped.
- Predicting of chronic offending is controversial.

IX. Delinquency the Life Course
- Life course criminology is concerned with explaining individual changes in offending throughout life.
- Relationship of anti-social behavior clusters to delinquency.
- Sampson and Laub contend *turning points* may lead to modifications in behavior.

A. Desistance from Crime
- *Desistance* is the age of termination from crime.
- Maturation towards pursing a conventional lifestyle (Glueck).
- Grove suggests biological and psychological factors play a major role in desistance
- Moffitt contends adolescent limiteds are situational will desist from crime over time compared to persisters who experienced early and long term antisocial behaviors.

KEY TERMS

age of onset   The age at which a youth performs their first criminal offense.

chronic youthful offenders   Youth involved in serious and repetitive offenses

cohort   A group of individuals having one or more statistical factors in common in a demographic study.

cohort study   Individuals who are usually born in a particular year in a particular city or county and studied by researchers throughout part or all of their lives.

desistance   The age at which an offender is no longer performing delinquent acts.

escalation of offenses   Offenses increase in severity from one age to the next.

hidden delinquency   Unobserved or unreported delinquency.

incidence of delinquency   Frequency of offending or the number of delinquent events.

juvenile court statistics   Records the number of children appearing before the court each year.

prevalence of delinquency   Refers to the number of young people involved in delinquent behavior.

reliability   The extent to which a questionnaire or interview yields the same results two or more times.

self-report studies   Studies that ask people to tell about crimes they may have committed in an earlier period of time.

specialization   Examines whether youths are involved in one or several types of delinquency.

turning point   Displays that some delinquents have a gradual or dramatic change to non-delinquent acts as they move into adulthood.

Uniform Crime Reports   The FBI's annual report of crimes committed in the United States.

Validity   Issue involving the accuracy of research data concerning self-report truthfulness.

victimization studies (NCVS) Surveys used to determine the extent of criminal victimization in the U.S. by asking people the nature of crimes perpetrated against them.

Practice Test

Multiple Choice:

1. The chapter begins with an interesting story involving the death of a _____.
a. 12 year old girl stolen from her bed room
b. 19 year old college women attacked on campus
c. college student working at a grocery store who was shot in a robbery
d. police officer in a large city
e. 3 year old boy

The murderer of the above victim was _____.
a. a 53 year old pedophile
b. a 22 year old college male
c. a member of the Gangster Disciples
d. a member of the Latin Kings
e. an 11 year old boy

2. The term incidence of delinquency refers to _____.
a. the person who committed the crime
b. the frequency of offending or the number of delinquent events.
c. the place where the crime occurred
d. the time of the crime
e. all of the above

3. The term prevalence of delinquency refers to _____.
a. the person who committed the crime
b. the place where the crime occurred
c. the number of young people involved in delinquent behavior
d. the time of the crime
e. all of the above

4. The crimes for which the FBI collects information are divided into two classes, Part I and Part II offenses. Part I offenses, are also know as _____.
a. important offenses
b. violent offenses
c. terrorists offenses
d. index offenses
e. felony offenses

5. The Part One Index offenses include all but one of the following _____.
a. murder
b. terrorism
c. rape
d. burglary
e. robbery

6. Which of the following is not included as a crime against the person in the part one offenses?
a. murder
b. terrorism
c. rape
d. aggravated assault
e. robbery

7. Which of the following in not included as a crime against property in the part one offenses?
a. embezzlement
b. burglary
c. larceny
d. auto theft
e. arson

8. A measure of investigative effectiveness that compares the number of crimes reported or discovered to the number of crimes solved through arrest or other means is called the _____.
a. prosecution rate
b. clearance rate
c. conviction rate
d. imprisonment rate
e. crime rate

9. The *Uniform Crime Report* _____.
a. vastly underestimates the actual amount of crime in the United States
b. vastly overestimates the actual amount of crime in the United States
c. predicts with great accuracy the amount of crime in the United States
d. is published by the University of Michigan
e. is published by the University of Illinois

10. During the term of President William Clinton, juvenile murder rates _____.
a. dramatically increased
b. increased, but just by a few percentage points
c. decreased, but just by a few percentage points
d. dramatically decreased
e. remained identical, no increase, no decrease

11. What percentage of juvenile arrest in 2005 were girls?
a. 5%
b. 10%
c. 15%
d. 20%
e. 25%

12. The most common form of murder in Britain is _____.
a. shootings with handguns
b. stabbings
c. poison
d. bludgeoning

13. Firearms account for _____ of all murders in Britain.
a. 9%
b. 19%
c. 29%
d. 39%
e. 49%

14. Firearms account for _____ of all murders in America.
a. 30%
b. 40%
c. 50%
d. 60%
e. 70%

15. In 1996, famous criminologist James Alan Fox predicted that _____.
a. violent youth crime would go up in 2005
b. violent youth crime would start to decline in 2005
c. violent youth crime would stabilize in 2005 and remain that way for at least ten years
d. violent youth crime would decline because of the number of youths in prison

16. A _____ is a group of individuals who are usually born in a particular year in a particular city or county and studied by researchers throughout part or all of their lives.
a. cohort study
b. friends study
c. neighborhood study
d. age specific study
e. peer group

17. Studies that ask people to tell about crimes they may have committed in an earlier period of time are called _____..
a. historical studies
b. self-report studies
c. cohort studies
d. friends studies
e. anthropological studies

18. Unobserved or unreported delinquency is also called _____.
a. reporting error
b. missing delinquency
c. hidden delinquency
d. missing delinquency
e. statistical lying

19. The extent to which a questionnaire or interview yields the same results two or more times is called _____..
a. dependability
b. validity
c. reliability
d. confidence factor
e. truth

20. The accuracy of research data concerning self-report truthfulness is referred to as _____..
a. dependability
b. validity
c. reliability
d. confidence factor
e. truth

21. Surveys used to determine the extent of criminal victimization in the U.S. by asking people the nature of crimes perpetrated against them are called .
a. history studies
b. Uniform Crime Report Studies
c. self report studies
d. record studies
e. victimization studies   (NCVS)

22. Victimization studies are usually conducted by the _____.
a. Federal Bureau of Investigation
b. Bureau of Justice Statistics
c. University of Illinois
d. Academy of Criminal Justice Sciences

23. Thomas McNulty and Paul Bellair found that _____ were involved in significantly lower, levels of serious violence than were whites.
a. whites
b. blacks
c. Hispanics
d. Native Americans
e. Asians

24. The age at which a youth performs their first criminal offense is called the _____.
a. age of onset
b. primary deviation
c. starting age
d. day of delinquency
e. the "first offense"

25. The term escalation of offenses means that _____.
a. the delinquent commits less crimes each year
b. offenses increase in severity from one age to the next.
c. the delinquent uses more marijuana each day
d. the delinquent spends more time in jail each year

True/False:

1. Juveniles who are arrested for Part II offenses are more likely to be held for trial as adults, whereas those arrested for Part I offenses are more likely to be tried as juveniles.

2. It is believed that the *Uniform Crime Reports* vastly underestimates the actual amount of crime in the United States.

3. During the term of President Bill Clinton, juvenile murder rates dramatically increased.

4. Like American policemen, British policemen are well armed.

5. In Britain, it is illegal for anyone under 16 to buy a knife.

6. Self-report studies have been particularly useful in helping researchers estimate the prevalence and incidence of drug use among adolescents in the United states

7. In a comparison of the National Crime Victimization Survey to the Uniform Crime Reports we find that the Uniform Crime Reports overestimate the number of juvenile victims in this country.

8. Studies based on official statistics have reported that African Americans are overrepresented in arrest, conviction, and incarceration relative to their population base.

9. Official statistics document that white females violate the law more frequently and more seriously than black females do.

10. Desistance is the age at which an offender is no longer performing delinquent acts.

Fill-in-the-blank:

1. The age at which a child begins to commit delinquent acts called _____

2. A juvenile who engages repeatedly in delinquent behavior is called _____.

3. The solution of a crime by arrest of a perpetrator who has confessed or who has been implicated by witnesses or evidence is called_____.

4. A generational group as defined in demographics, statistics, or for the purpose of social research is called a _____.

5. Research that usually includes all individuals who were born in a particular year in a particular city or county and follows them through part or all of their lives is called a _____.

6. The termination of a delinquent career or behavior is called _____.

7. An increase in the frequency and severity of an individual's offenses; an important dimension of delinquency is sometimes referred to as an _____.

8. Unobserved or unreported delinquency.

9. The frequency with which delinquent behavior takes place.

10. The most serious offenses reported by the FBI in the *Uniform Crime Reports,* including murder and nonnegligent manslaughter, forcible rape, robbery, aggravated assault, burglary, larceny-theft, motor vehicle theft, and arson are called the _____.

11. Data about youth who appear before the juvenile court, compiled annually by the National Center for Juvenile Justice is called _____

12. The percentage of the juvenile population who are involved in delinquent behavior is referred to as the _____.

13. The extent to which a questionnaire or interview yields the same answers from the same juveniles when they are questioned two or more times is called _____.

14. Studies of juvenile crime based on surveys in which youth report on their own delinquent acts is called _____.

15. Repeated involvement of a juvenile in one type of delinquency during the course of his or her offending is sometimes referred to as _____.

16. A gradual or dramatic change in the trajectory of an individual's life course is called a _____.

17. The Federal Bureau of Investigation's annual statistical reports of crimes committed in the United States is entitled the _____.

18. The extent to which a research instrument measures what it claims it measures is called _____.

19. Ongoing surveys of crime victims in the United States conducted by the Bureau of Justice Statistics to determine the extent of crime is referred to as _____.

Essay Questions:

1. Delinquent behavior can be described along four different dimensions. Explain each of those dimensions.

2. Your text gives six majors findings by the *Uniform crime Reports* about juveniles. What are those six findings?

3. Explain the situation of knives and crime I Great Britain according to your text.

4. How do self-report studies work?

5. How does the National Crime victimization study work? How are its findings different from the Uniform Crime Report? Which one is more reliable?

6. How does the issue of race affect juvenile arrests and crime statistics?

7. Describe the concept of desistance and explain how it works.

Answers Practice Test

Multiple Choice:
1. Answer: e; e   2. Answer: b   3. Answer: c   4. Answer: d   5. Answer: b   6. Answer: b
7. Answer: a   8. Answer: b   9. Answer: a   10. Answer: d   11. Answer: d   12. Answer: b
13. Answer: a   14. Answer: e   15. Answer: a   16. Answer: a   17. Answer: b
18. Answer: c   19. Answer: c   20. Answer: b   21. Answer: e   22. Answer: b
23. Answer: e   24. Answer: a   25. Answer: b

True/False:
1. False   2. True   3. False   4. False   5. True   6. True   7. False   8. True   9. False
10. True

Fill-in-the-blank:
1. age of onset
2. chronic youthful offender
3. clearance by arrest
4. cohort
5. cohort study
6. desistance
7. escalation of offenses
8. hidden delinquency
9. incidence of delinquency
10. Index offenses
11. juvenile court statistics
12. prevalence of delinquency
13. reliability
14. self-report studies
15. specialization
16. turning point
17. *Uniform Crime Reports*
18. validity
19. victimization studies

LECTURE OUTLINE

Introduction

- Attempted murder by a high school junior of her own child.

I. The Classical School and Delinquency
- Montesquieu began the debate of government's role in punishment of criminals
- Beccaria viewed the legitimacy of criminal sanctions based on the *social contract*.
- Bentham viewed contended punishment would deter persons from crime based on rationality.
- Punishment should: (1) prevent all offenses, (2) persuade those committing offenses to commit less serious ones, (3) do no more mischief than necessary, and (4) prevent crime at a cheap cost.
- The doctrine of *free will* and *utilitarianism* of punishment.
- *Felicific calculus* of balancing pleasure and pain.

II. The Rationality of Crime
- Ecological research and selection of suitable crime targets by rational offenders.
- Economic analysis and responses to incentives and deterrents by rational decision making.

A. Rational Choice Theory
- Cook's *criminal opportunity theory*; targets that offer the highest payoff with smallest amount of risk.
- Cohen/Felson's routine activity approach; increase in suitable targets and decrease in guardians, presence of motivated offenders.
- Association of rationality and free will.
- Some studies suggest delinquent behavior is largely not planned, but spur-of-the-moment.
- Youngsters appear not to be able to control emotions as exemplified in compulsive behaviors.
- Influence of peer groups may lead youngsters to bypass a rational process.

B. Is Delinquent Behavior Rational?
- Antisocial behavior often appears purposeful and rational.
- Persistent offenders often desist from crime as they mature.
- Many youth do not exhibit signs of having free will to commit crime, especially when many delinquent acts are impulsive in nature.
- Robert Agnew suggests freedom of choice varies from one individual to another depending on biological, psychological, and sociological factors.

III. Positivism and Delinquency

A. Development of Positivism
- The causes of human behavior can be modified to eliminate societal problems.
- *Positivism* dominant philosophy at beginning of twentieth century (Progressive era).
- Three assumptions: (1) backgrounds of individuals explain behaviors, (2) behavior is determined by prior causes, and (3) the delinquent is fundamentally different.

B. Early Theories of Biological Positivism
- Nature v. nurture debate.
- Lombroso and the *born criminal* (atavistic).
- Theory could not stand test of scientific investigation (Ferri and Goring).

- Lombroso's contributions include studying individuals and using control groups.
- Goddard's genealogical study of *feebleminded boys* and "badstock."
- Sheldon and body types; *endomorphic, mesomorphic, ectomorphic*.
- Mesomorphic more likely to be delinquent (most aggressive of the types)
- Sheldon's work cited for numerous flaws, too subjective and inaccurate.

C. Sociobiology and Contemporary Biological Positivism

- Stresses interaction between biological factors and influence of environments.
- Relationship of identical twins and adoption studies to delinquency.
- West/Farrington and IQ studies characterize criminals as having low IQ's.
- Wilson/Herrnstein suggested an inverse relationship between school and IQ.
- Eysenck and *autonomic nervous system*, suggesting that *extroverts* are more difficult to condition than *introverts*. Extroverts more likely to be involved with delinquency.
- Moffit's developmental theory: (1) develops lifelong paths at early age (LCP), and (2) develops during adolescent years (AL) delinquents.
- Kandel/Mednick and study of Danish birth cohort suggest pregnancy/delivery events predicted adult violent offending.
- Difficulty of children staying on task and hyperactivity due to attention deficit disorder with hyperactivity (ADHD).
- Learning disabilities (LD) impede learning and may be linked to delinquency.
- Orthomolecular deficits and excesses may contribute to delinquency.

D. Psychological Positivism

- Freud; (1) personality has three components, (2) three psychosexual stages of development, and (3) personality traits developed in early childhood.
- The *id* (primitive drives), *ego* and *superego* (controlling agents of the id)
- Freud's four constructs; (1) delinquent behavior is related to neurotic personality development, (2) defective superego, (3) overdeveloped superego, and (4) fixation in early stages lead to lifelong searches for gratification.
- Hindelang suggests delinquents are pleasure-seekers more than nondelinquents and willing to take a risk for the sake of such experiences.
- Katz's *Seduction of Crime* purports an emotional process of seduction and compulsion.
- According to Katz, crimes are sensually compelling for some delinquents.
- Glueck's personality of delinquents are defiant, ambivalent about authority, extroverted, fearful of failure, resentful, hostile, suspicious, and defensive.
- Psychopaths (*sociopaths*) are undomesticated children with no sense of trust in adults.
- Wilson/Herrnstein's *reinforcement theory*; rewards of crime are found in material gain, revenge against an enemy, peer approval, and sexual gratification. Critics of Wilson/Herrnstein say they factor society out of their consideration of crime.
- Developmental Theories of delinquency
- Moffit's Trajectories of Offending
- Tremblay's Trajectories of Offending
- The Cambridge Study of delinquent Development

KEY TERMS

attention deficit disorder Disorder of children that can include inattention, distractibility, excessive activity, restlessness, noisiness, and impulsiveness.

autonomic nervous system Hans Eysenks's theory that holds that there is a relationship between delinquency and both biological and environmental factors, affecting extroverts and introverts differently.

biological positivism The belief that biological limitations may lead juveniles to delinquency.

born criminal Lombroso claimed some criminals are atavistic or a reversion to an earlier evolutionary level.

criminal opportunity theory Phillip J. Cook suggests that criminals tend to be attracted to targets that offer high payoffs with little risk of legal consequences.

determinism A view that an individual's acts are determined by a preexisting biological, psychological, or sociological condition beyond the individual's control.

emotionality An aspect of temperament; can range from near absence of emotional response to intense, out-of-control emotions.

felicific calculus A notion that holds that human beings are oriented toward obtaining a favorable balance of pleasure and pain.

free will A belief purported by the *Classical School of Criminology* which holds that juveniles are rational creatures who are free to choose their own actions and therefore should be held responsible for their behavior.

learning disabilities Disorders in one or more of the basic psychological processes involved in understand or using spoken or written language. Some support exists for a theorized link between juvenile delinquency and learning disabilities.

orthomolecular imbalances Chemical imbalances in the body, resulting from poor nutrition, allergies, and exposure to lead and certain other substances, which are said to lead to delinquency.

positivism The view that once human behavior can be understood in a scientific sense, that behavior can be modified to eliminate many of society's problems, such as delinquency.

Progressive Era The period from around 1890 to 1920 , when a wave of optimism swept through American society and led to the acceptance of positivism. The emerging social sciences assured reformers that through positivism society's problems could be solved.

progressivism The belief that through positivism society can be improved.

psychoanalysis   Techniques developed by psychologists for examining the subconscious and how it relates to human behavior.

psychoanalytic theory   Sigmund Freud's insights. Which have helped shape the handling of juvenile delinquents. They include these axioms: (1) the personality is made up of three components-id, ego, and superego; (2) all normal children pass through three psychosexual stages of development-oral, anal, and phallic; and (3) a person's personality traits are developed in early childhood.

reinforcement theory   Wilson and Herrnstein's theory that suggests that behavior is governed by its consequences of rewards and punishments.

routine activity approach   Lawrence E. Cohen and Marcus Felson contend that crime rate trends and cycles are affected by the routine activity structure of American society.

social contract   A view that purports humans are rational creatures willing to surrender enough liberty to the state, so that society can establish sanctions for the preservation of social order.

sociobiology   An expression of biological positivism that stresses interaction between biological factors within an individual and the influence of a particular environment.

sociopath   Emotionally deprived children with little or no sense of remorse who frequently become delinquent. Also referred to as psychopaths within the discipline of psychology.

trait-based personality models   Theories that attribute delinquent behavior to an individual's basic, inborn personal characteristics.

utilitarianism   A doctrine which holds that the useful is the good, and that the aim of social or political action should be the greatest good for the greatest number.

Practice Test

Multiple Choice

1. The vignette at the beginning of the chapter is about _____.
a. infanticide
b. homicide
c. suicide
d. a murder at a grocery store
e. drug sells

2. The view that delinquents cannot stop themselves from committing crime because of some overpowering influence is called _____.
a. utilitarianism
b. positivism
c. determinism
d. free-will
e. free-choice

3. The view that humans act as rational creatures were willing to surrender enough liberty to the state so that society can establish rules and sanctions for the preservation of the social order was held by _____.
a. Charles de Secondat
b. Baron de Montesquieu
c. Cesare Beccaria
d. Jeremy Bentham
e. All of the above

4. Who is the author of the 1747 book entitled *On the Spirit of the Laws*?
a. Charles de Secondat
b. Baron de Montesquieu
c. Cesare Beccaria
d. Jeremy Bentham
e. Cesare Lombroso

5. Who's the author of the 1764 book entitled *On Crime and Punishments*?
a. Charles de Secondat
b. Baron de Montesquieu
c. Cesare Beccaria
d. Jeremy Bentham
e. Cesare Lombroso

6. A doctrine that holds that the useful is the good, and that the aim of social or political action should be the greatest good for the greatest number is called _____.
a. utilitarianism
b. positivism
c. determinism
d. free-will
e. free-choice

7. Who wrote that punishment "should be public, immediate, and necessary; the least possible of the case given; proportion to the crime and determined by the laws"?
a. Charles de Secondat
b. Baron de Montesquieu
c. Cesare Beccaria
d. Jeremy Bentham
e. Cesare Lombroso

8. Who wrote, in 1780, *An Introduction to the Principles of Morals and Legislation*?
a. Charles de Secondat
b. Baron de Montesquieu
c. Cesare Beccaria
d. Jeremy Bentham
e. Cesare Lombroso

9. A notion that holds that human beings are oriented toward obtaining a favorable balance of pleasure and pain is called _____.
a. positivism
b. determinism
c. indeterminism
d. criminology
e. felicific calculus

10. Phillip J. Cook suggests that criminals tend to be attracted to targets that offer high payoffs with little risk of legal consequences is called _____?
a. learning theory
b. psychoanalytic theory
c. reinforcement theory
d. criminal opportunity theory
e. felicific calculus

11. Lawrence E. Cohen and Marcus Felson contend that crime rate trends and cycles are affected by the routine activity structure of American society is called _____.
a. learning theory
b. psychoanalytic theory
c. routine activities approach
d. criminal opportunity theory
e. felicific calculus

12. Lawrence E. Cohen and Marcus Felson believe that the volume and distribution of predatory crime is related to _____.
a. the availability of suitable targets
b. the absence of capable guardians
c. the presence of motivated offenders
d. all of the above

13. Which of the following writers would most likely believe that crime is a rational choice?
a. Ernest van den Haag
b. Cesare Lombroso
c. Emile Durkheim
d. Robert Merton
e. All of the above

14. According to the text, why is it that in youth gangs they sometimes allow the youngest member to do the beatings during a mugging?
a. he is the toughest gang member
b. since he is small, it is harder to hit him
c. since he is under 15, the gang members know he'll be back on the streets in no time
d. since he is small, he is able to sneak up on the person

15. The view that once human behavior can be understood in a scientific sense, that behavior can be modified to eliminate many of society's problems, such as delinquency is called

_____.
a. positivism
b. criminal justice
c. indeterminism
d. criminology
e. felicific calculus

16. The Progressive Era was from _____.
a. 1776-1792
b. 1810-1830
c. 1861-1889
d. 1890-1920
e. 1960-1982

17. A view that an individual's acts are determined by a preexisting biological, psychological, or sociological condition beyond the individual's control is called _____.
a. positivism
b. determinism
c. indeterminism
d. criminology
e. felicific calculus

18. The idea that one can discern the inner qualities of a person through outward appearances of their face is called _____.
a. phrenology
b. physiognomy
c. hedonistic calculus
d. indeterminism
e. psychological adaptation

19. A conditioned characterized by the existence of features thought to be common in earlier stages of human evolution is called _____.
a. heredity
b. moral depravity
c. atavism
d. psychological mal-adaptation
e. mental illness

20. Who is considered to be the Father of the Biological School of Criminology?
a. Charles de Secondat
b. Baron de Montesquieu
c. Cesare Beccaria
d. Jeremy Bentham
e. Cesare Lombroso

21. Who is considered to be the Father of the Classical School of Criminology?
a. Charles de Secondat
b. Baron de Montesquieu
c. Cesare Beccaria
d. Jeremy Bentham
e. Cesare Lombroso

22. Which of the following authors considered criminals to be a reversion to an earlier evolutionary form of primitive man?
a. Charles de Secondat
b. Baron de Montesquieu
c. Cesare Beccaria
d. Jeremy Bentham
e. Cesare Lombroso

23. Cesare Lombroso came to his startling conclusions while _____.
a. working in a prison in Milan
b. examining a crime scene in Rome
c. examining the skull of the notorious criminal Vihella
d. having a conversation with Cesare Beccaria
e. attending the execution of Socrates

24. In 1877, Richard Dugdale did a detailed genealogical study of the _____ family.
a. Smith
b. Kallikak
c. Burroughs
d. Jukes
e. Shaw

25. In 1913, Henry Goddard conducted a well-known genealogical study for _____ boys and girls.
a. psychologically disturbed
b. feeble minded
c. atavistic
d. uneducated
e. unemployable

26. Who was the author of *Varieties of Delinquent Behavior*?
a. William Sheldon
b. Cesare Lombroso
c. Cesare Beccaria
d. Jeremy Bentham
e. Richard Dugdale

27. Which of the following body types in not one that Sheldon described?
a. mesomorphic
b. endomorphic
c. metamorphic
d. ectomorphic

28. Which book by Sheldon and Eleanor Glueck was the result of comprehensive research into persistent delinquency?
a. *Physique and Delinquency*
b. *Ventures in Criminology*
c. *Identification and Predelinquency*
d. *Predicting Delinquency and Crime*
e. *Crime and Justice*

29. In Sheldon and Eleanor Glueck's study, what percent of the delinquents were mesmorphic?
a. 28.9%
b. 60.1%
c. 92.5%
d. 43.7%
e. 30.7%

30. The interaction between the biological factors within an individual and the influence of the particular environment is called _____.
a. psychology
b. criminology
c. sociology
d. anthropology
e. sociobiology

True/False

1. According to many philosophers of natural law, human behavior is merely one facet of a universe that is part of a natural order.

2. Sheldon found that delinquents were more likely to be ectomorphic and less likely to be mesomorphic.

3. Cesare Beccaria is best remember for his writings on the Positive School f Criminology.

4. Cesare Lombroso is best remembered for his writings on the classical School of Criminology.

5. The author of *On the Spirit of the Laws* is Baron de Montesquieu.

6. Cesare Beccaria felt that punishment should be maximized and severe in each case.

7. Utilitarianism is doctrine which holds that the useful is the good, and that the aim of social or political action should be the greatest good for the greatest number.

8. Sometimes sociopaths are referred to as emotionally deprived children with little or no sense of remorse who frequently become delinquent.

9. Positivism is the view that once human behavior can be understood in a scientific sense, that behavior can be modified to eliminate many of society's problems, such as delinquency.

10. The Progressive era occurred during the 1960s producing much change in the juvenile justice system.

Fill-in-the-blank:

1. A cognitive disorder of childhood that can include inattention, distractibility excessive activity, restlessness, noisiness, impulsiveness, and so on is called

_____.

2. The system of nerves that govern reflexes, glands, the iris of the eye, and activities of inferior organs that are not subject to voluntary control is called the _____.

3. The belief that juveniles' biological characteristics and limitations drive them to delinquent behavior is sometimes called _____.

4. According to Cesare Lombroso, an individual who is atavistic, or reverts to an earlier evolutionary level and is unable to conform his or her behavior to the requirements of modern society is called a _____

5. A theory claiming that criminals tend to be attracted to targets that offer a high payoff with little risk of legal consequences is _____.

6. _____ is a philosophical position that suggests that individuals are driven into delinquent or criminal behavior by biological or psychological traits that are beyond their control.

7. An aspect of temperament' that can range from a near absence of emotional response to intense, out-of-control emotional reactions is called _____.

8. A method for determining the sum total of pleasure and pain produced by an act, Also, the assumption that human beings strive to obtain a favorable balance of pleasure and pain is called _____.

9. The ability to make rational choices among possible actions, and to select one over the others is called _____.

10. Chemical imbalances in the body, resulting from poor nutrition, allergies, and exposure to lead and certain other substances, which are said to lead to delinquency are referred to as

_____

11. The view that, just as laws operate in the medical, biological, and physical sciences, laws govern human behavior; and that these laws can be understood and used is called

_____.

12. The period from around 1890 to 1920, when a wave of optimism swept through American society and led to the acceptance of positivism. The emerging social sciences assured reformers that through positivism society's problems could be solved. This era is called the

_____

13. Sigmund Freud's insights, which have helped shape the handing of juvenile delinquents. They include these axioms: (1) the personality is made up of three components-id, ego, and superego; (2) all normal children pass through three psychosexual stages of development-oral, anal, and phallic; and (3) a person's personality traits are developed in early childhood. This is called _____.

14. A youth with a personality disorder and is a hard juvenile criminal. The claim is made that the _____ or _____ is the unwanted, rejected child who grows up but remains an undomesticated child and never develops trust in or loyalty to another person.

15. A perspective that holds that behavior is governed by its consequences especially rewards and punishments to follow from it is called _____.

16. Lawrence E. Cohen and Marcus Felson's contention that crime rate trends and cycles are related to the nature of everyday patterns of social interaction that characterize the society in which they occur is called _____.

17. An unstated or explicit agreement between a people and its government as to the rights and obligations of each is called a _____

18. An expression of biological positivism that stresses the interaction between biological factors within an individual and the influence of the person's particular environment. The systematic study of the biological basis of all social behavior is called _____.

20. Theories that attribute delinquent behavior to an individuals basic; inborn characteristics are called _____.

21. A doctrine which holds that the useful is the good, and that the aim of social or political action should be the greatest good for the greatest number is called _____

22. Disorders in one or more of the basic psychological processes involved in understanding or using spoken or written language are called _____.

Essay:

1. What are the basic theoretical constructs of the classical school of criminology?

2. Jeremy Bentham stated that punishment has 4 objectives. What are those 4 objectives?

3. John Conrad tells the sad story of Billy in this chapter. Write an essay about Billy's sad world.

4. Explain the concept of routine activities theory.

5. The positive approach to youth crime is based on 3 basic assumptions. Explain each of those assumptions..

Multiple Choice:

1. Answer: a   2. Answer: c   3. Answer: e   4. Answer: b   5. Answer: c   6. Answer: a
7. Answer: c   8. Answer: d   9. Answer: e   10. Answer: d   11. Answer: d   12. Answer: d
13. Answer: a   14. Answer: c   15. Answer: a   16. Answer: d   17. Answer: b
18. Answer: b   19. Answer: c   20. Answer: e   21. Answer: c   22. Answer: e
23. Answer: c   24. Answer: d   25. Answer: b   26. Answer: a   27: Answer: d
28. Answer: a   29. Answer: b   30. Answer: b

True/False:

1. True   2. False   3. False   4. False   5. True   6. False   7. True   8. True   9. True
10. False

Fill-in-the-blank:

1. Attention Deficit Hyperactivity Disorder (ADHD)
2. automatic nervous system
3. biological positivism
4. born criminal
5. criminal opportunity theory
6. Determinism
7. emotionality
8. felicific calculus
9. free will
10. Orthomolecular imbalances
11. Positivism
12. Progressive Era
13. Psychoanalytic Theory
14. psychopath or sociopath
15. Reinforcement theory
16. Routine activities approach
17. social contract
18. sociobiology
19. trait-based personality models
20. Utilitarianism
21. Learning Disabilities (LDs)

WEBSITES

www.aecr.org   To learn more about the Annie E. Casey Foundation.

www.wholechild.net

www.utilitarinaism.com/mill1.htm   To learn more about utilitarianism.

www.pbs.org/wgbh/pages/frontline/angel   To learn more about Ernest van den Haag.

CHAPTER 4: SOCIAL STRUCTURAL THEORIES

LEARNING OBJECTIVES

After reading this chapter, you should be able to answer the following questions:

1. How is cultural deviance theory related to lower-class delinquency?

2. What is the relationship between socially disorganized communities and delinquent behavior?

3. How does strain propel juveniles into delinquency behavior?

4. What delinquent behavior explains homelessness among youth?

CHAPTER SUMMARY

This chapter describes the importance of ecological theories in explaining delinquency. Shaw and McKay, members of the *Chicago School*, showed an association of where a young person lives as having an impact on delinquency. The closer youths live to the inner city, the more likely they are to become involved in delinquency (*social disorganization*). The explanation for the delinquency in these areas goes beyond that of social disorganization, for a cultural tradition passes these criminogenic norms from one generation to the next.

Merton's social structure and anomie theory states that the social structure of a society influences the behavior that occurs within the society. Youths who are caught in *anomie* or normlessness are more likely to become delinquent. Albert Cohen's theory of lower-class gang cultures (*status frustration*), was influenced by the work of Merton. Cohen suggested that lower-class youth aspire to middle-class values, but their inability to attain them causes an inversion of values in which youths engage in delinquent behavior. Similarly, Cloward and Ohlin argue that youths become involved in delinquent behavior when unable to attain legitimate pursuits and are therefore forced to pursue illegitimate avenues. Conversely, Miller suggests that lower-class youths do not aspire to middle-class values, rather they develop their own set of *focal concerns* which encourage delinquent behavior.

The context of all these theories relates to the structure of society. The structural theories view delinquency as a response to social inequalities. They vary in the mechanisms they describe as mediating the impact of inequalities, but their focus is still to identify an explanation to help one understand delinquent behavior. Social structural theories propose that structural and cultural disorder results in high rates of crime, unsafe and disruptive living conditions, and the breeding ground for unsocialized individuals who strike out against society.

LECTURE OUTLINE

Introduction:
- Four Harlem teenagers accused of murder.

I. Social Disorganization Theory
- Durkheim *anomie/normlessness* resulting from society's failure to regulate its member's attitudes and behaviors.

A. Shaw and McKay
- Shaw and McKay focused on social characteristic of the community.
- Delinquency results from breakdown of social control among primary groups.
- Influences of rapid industrialization, urbanization, and immigration.
- Burgess/Park and *The Chicago School* focus on ecology.
- Burgess and *concentric zones* and relationship to delinquency.
- Shaw/McKay find economic and occupational structure influences delinquency and class position in society.
- *Cultural transmission* of delinquent values from generation to the next.
- The theory lost vitality in the late 1960s, but resurfaced in the 1980s.
- Shaw/McKay influenced multiple levels of analysis and shifted focus on delinquency away from individual and to the larger community.
- *Chicago Area Projects* aimed at reducing delinquency.

B. Evaluation of Shaw and McKay's Disorganization Theory
- The theory provided insight into how people and institutions adapt to their environment
- Critics charge delinquency is viewed as both an example and cause of disorganization
- Delinquency in America: Cities Grapple with Crime by Kids
- Social Policy 4.2 Project on Human Development in Chicago Neighborhoods

II. Cultural Deviance Theory and Delinquency
- View delinquency as an expression of conformity to opposing values and norms.

A. Miller's Lower-Class Culture and Delinquent Values
- *Focal concerns* of the lower-class: trouble, toughness, smartness, excitement, fate, and autonomy.
- Physical prowess is demonstrated by strength and endurance.
- Smartness is necessary to achieve material goods and personal status.
- Search for excitement and thrill typically from alcohol and gambling.
- Social forces over which individuals have little control leads to their destiny.
- Miller contends the lower-class have a distinctive culture of their own.
- One-sex peer groups are a significant structural form in the lower-class community.

B. Evaluation of Miller's Thesis
- Critics charge not all youths are affected by the same subculture values.

- Some youth hold the values and norms of the dominant culture.

III. Strain and Delinquency
- Views delinquency as a consequence of frustration when persons are unable to achieve the goals they desire.

A. Merton's Theory of Anomie
- *Culturally defined goals* as legitimate objectives for society.
- *Institutional means* to achieve the goals are acceptable.
- When culture lacks integration, a state of normlessness/*anomie* occurs.
- Typologies of adaptation; conformity, innovation, ritualism, retreatism, and rebellion.

B. Evaluation of Merton's Theory
- Recent research suggests the predictive power of strain theory has been underestimated

C. Strain Theory and the Individual Level of Analysis
- Research has suggested strain is a better predictor of delinquency than financial goals
- Agnew's revised *general strain theory* with three sources of strain: 1) failure to achieve valued goals, 2) removal of positive stimuli, and 3) presentation of negative stimuli.

D. Cohen's Theory of Delinquent Subcultures
- Lower-class youths are protesting against middle-class goals.
- Experience *status frustration* when unable to achieve the goals.
- *Reaction formation* is used to cope with status frustration.
- Delinquent subculture offers status to lower-class males.
- Nonutilitarian crimes are committed "for the hell of it."
- Subculture characterized by "short-run hedonism."

E. Evaluation of Cohens' Theory
- Cohen's theory views delinquency as a process of interaction.
- Critics charge most delinquent boys become law abiding even though their lower-class status does not change.

F. Cloward and Ohlin's Opportunity Theory
- Conceptualized success and status as separate strivings operating independently of each other.
- Type I and Type II boys are striving to increase their status and values are consistent with the middle-class.
- Type IV tend to avoid conflicts with middle-class institutions and authorities.
- Type III experience greatest conflict and are most likely to be delinquent.
- Criminal subculture based on illegal acts of extortion/fraud/theft for success.
- Conflict subculture consists of violence, force/threats to gain status or "rep."
- Retreatist subculture is concerned with drugs for gaining the "kick."

G. **Evaluation of Cloward and Ohlin's Theory**
  - Critics suggest lower class delinquents may not be talented people with lack of legitimate opportunities, rather delinquents may have limited social and intellectual abilities with low expectations and low aspirations.

IV. **Social Stratification and Delinquency**
  - A youth may become delinquent because they live in a disorganized community.
  - Class is a significant variable, however some challenge that association.
  - Coleman's *social capital theory* suggests lower-class individuals lack the social resources such as social norms, social networks, and interpersonal relationships that contribute to child growth.

V. **Explanations of Delinquency Across the Life Course**

  A. **Reduced Social Capital**
   - Lower-class forced to struggle to meet their basic survival needs.
   - The inability to meet goals encourages adolescents to pursue illegitimate means.

  B. **Disorganized Communities**
   - Lower-class must deal with cultural patterns conducive to delinquent behavior.
   - *Collective efficacy* relates to informal social control, cohesion and mutual trust.

  C. **Agency and Structure**
   - Recent evidence supports a relationship between agency and structure.
   - Critics contend structural and cultural theories do not explain some youths not becoming delinquent when in the same social setting and economic situations.

KEY TERMS

blocked opportunity   Limitation of legitimate opportunities to improve one's economic position which may result in a person turning to delinquent behavior.

Chicago Area Projects   A community organization project developed by Shaw and McKay in the 1930s to reduce the incidence of delinquency.

cultural deviance theory   View that delinquent behavior is an expression of conformity to cultural values that conflict with dominant values of the larger society.

cultural transmission theories   These theories contend that delinquent values are transmitted within a culture over time and from one generation to the next.

culturally defined goals   Merton's concept of goals that people feel are worth striving for and are held out as legitimate objectives for all members of society.

differential opportunity structure   Shaw/McKay's analysis that economic and social disorganization within a community are influential to delinquency.

focal concerns   Miller contends that lower-class youths have different value subsets from those of the middle-class values (toughness, smartness, excitement, fate, and autonomy).

institutional means   Merton's concept of acceptable methods which people achieve the culturally defined goals of society.

opportunity theory   Cloward and Ohlin's theory which purports that individuals will pursue illegitimate pathways if legitimate opportunities are not available to them within society.

reaction formation   A defense mechanism used to handle status frustration where the delinquent directs irrational hostility toward the middle-class.

social capital   Coleman's theoretical construct that lower-class individuals have higher rates of delinquency due to lack of norms, social networks, and interpersonal relationships that contribute to a child's growth.

social disorganization   Shaw and McKay's view that delinquency results from the breakdown of social control among traditional primary groups, such as family, neighborhood, and the social disorganization of the community.

social structure   The relatively stable formal and informal arrangements that characterize society-including its economic arrangements, social institutions and its values and norms.

status frustration   Cohen's theoretical construct that lower-class youths protest middle-class values and feel social strain when they are unable to achieve those values.

strain theory   A theory that proposes that the pressure of social structure pushes youths into nonconforming behavior when they are unable to attain the cultural goal of success.

Practice Test

Multiple Choice:

1. In the vignette at the beginning of this chapter, four Harlem teenagers were accused of
_____.
a. a murder
b. a rape
c. a suicide
d. a car accident
e. possessing drugs

2. The relatively stable formal and informal arrangements that characterize society-including its economic arrangements, social institutions and its values and norms is called _____.
a. strain theory
b. social disorganization theory
c. social structure
d. blocked opportunity
e. reaction formation

3. Shaw and McKay's view that delinquency results from the breakdown of social control among traditional primary groups, such as family, neighborhood, and the social disorganization of the community is called _____.
a. strain theory
b. social disorganization theory
c. social structure
d. blocked opportunity
e. reaction formation

4. In Durkheim's view, anomie or "normlessness" resulted from _____.
a. too much influence by religion
b. parents having too much control over their children
c. democratic institutions
d. a strong central government
e. society's failure to provide adequate regulation of its members attitudes and behaviors

5. Elijah Anderson's *Code of the Streets* grew out of the ethnographic work Anderson did in two urban communities in _____.
a. Chicago
b. Los Angeles
c. Seattle
d. Philadelphia
e. New York

6. Social disorganization theory was developed by Clifford R. Shaw and Henry D. McKay who attended _____.
a. Harvard University
b. Boston College
c. University of Chicago
d. West Virginia University
e. University of Michigan

7. _____ and _____ had used the concept of ecology in explaining the growth of cities.
a. Shaw, McKay
b. Durkheim, Anderson
c. Miller, Cohen
d. Park, Burgess
e. Cloward, Ohlin

8. In _____ Shaw and McKay published their classic work *Juvenile Delinquency and Urban Areas*.
a. 1932
b. 1938
c. 1942
d. 1947
e. 1951

9. Robert J. Sampson developed the concept of _____ as characteristics of a community that would work together to prevent and control crime.
a. anomie theory
b. symbolic interactionism
c. collective efficacy
d. conflict theory
e. Marxist theory

10. Which of the following is a characteristic of efficacy?
a. residents have mutual trust
b. residents have shared values
c. residents have a disposition to intervene for the public good.
d. all of the above

11. Walter B. Miller called the capacity to outsmart, outfox, outwit, con, dupe, and take others _____.
a. trouble
b. toughness
c. smartness
d. excitement
e. autonomy

12. Lower-class individuals often feel that their lives are subject to a set of forces over which they have little control. Miller called this _____.
a. trouble
b. toughness
c. smartness
d. excitement
e. fate

13. Walter B. Miller said that physical prowess as demonstrated as strength and endurance is valued in lower class culture. Miller called this characteristic _____.
a. trouble
b. toughness
c. smartness
d. excitement
e. fate

14. Miller called the desire for personal independence _____.
a. trouble
b. toughness
c. smartness
d. excitement
e. autonomy

15. _____ proposes that delinquency results from the frustration individuals feel when they are unable to achieve the goals they desire.
a. strain theory
b. conflict theory
c. functional theory
d. symbolic interaction theory
e. economic theory

16. When a person rejects a cultural and the institutional means and replaces them with new cultural goals and institutional means it is called _____.
a. conformity
b. innovation
c. ritualism
d. retreatism
e. rebellion

17. When a person agrees with the cultural goals and the institutional means that is called

_____.

a. conformity
b. innovation
c. ritualism
d. retreatism
e. rebellion

18. Richard Merton's revision of _____ has been called "the most influential single formulation in the sociology of deviance in the last 25 years and … possibly the most frequently quoted single paper in modern sociology."

a. strain theory
b. conflict theory
c. anomie theory
d. symbolic interaction theory
e. economic theory

19. Cohen's theoretical construct that lower-class youths protest middle-class values and feel social strain when they are unable to achieve those values is called _____.

a. status frustration
b. focal concerns
c. opportunity
d. reaction formation
e. blocked opportunity

20. A defense mechanism used to handle status frustration where the delinquent directs irrational hostility toward the middle-class is called _____.

a. status frustration
b. focal concerns
c. opportunity
d. reaction formation
e. blocked opportunity

21. Who suggested that juvenile delinquents commit crimes "for the hell of it".

a. Robert Merton
b. Albert Cohen
c. Richard Cloward
d. Lloyd Ohlin
e. David Matza

22. What subculture is primarily based on criminal values?
a. violent subculture
b. retreatist subculture
c. conflict subculture
d. terrorist subculture
e. criminal subculture

23. Violence is the key ingredient in the _____, whose members pursue status through force or threats of force.
a. violent subculture
b. retreatist subculture
c. conflict subculture
d. terrorist subculture
e. criminal subculture

24. The consumption of drugs is the basic activity of the _____.
a. violent subculture
b. retreatist subculture
c. conflict subculture
d. terrorist subculture
e. criminal subculture

25. Coleman's theoretical construct that lower-class individuals have higher rates of delinquency due to lack of norms, social networks, and interpersonal relationships that contribute to a child's growth is called _____.
a. strain theory
b. cultural transmission theory
c. opportunity theory
d. social capital theory
e. social disorganization theory

True/False:

1. "Manhood on the street implies physicality and a certain ruthlessness."

2. Walter B. Miller argued that the motivation to become involved in delinquent behavior endemic to middle-class culture.

3. Robert Merton argued that a set of focal concerns of the lower-class was related to criminal activity.

4. A main emphasis on Merton's theory is that it is "a theory of societal 'anomie', not of individually felt strain."

5. Merton's theoretical construct that lower-class individuals have higher rates of delinquency due to lack of norms, social networks, and interpersonal relationships that contribute to a child's growth is called social capital theory.

6. Drugs is the key ingredient of the criminal subculture.

7. Cloward and Ohlin's opportunity theory has been criticized because it portrays gang delinquents as talented youth who have a sense of injustice about the lack of legitimate opportunities available to them.

8. There has been a lack of interest among sociological theorists in the relationship between agency and structure.

9. Five types of individual adaptation are conformity, innovation, ritualism, retreatism, and rebellion.

10. Social disorganization theory was developed by Shaw and McKay at New York University.

Fill-in-the-blank:

1. According to strain theory, limited or nonexistent chances of success are called

_____.

2. A theory promoted by Clifford R. Shaw, Henry D. McKay, and Walter B. Miller, who view delinquent behavior as an expression of conformity to cultural values and norms that are in opposition to those of the larger U.S. society is called

_____.

3. The is an approach which holds that areas of concentrated crime maintain their high rates over a long period, even when the composition of the population changes rapidly, because delinquent "values" become cultural norms and are passed from one generation to the next is called _____.

4. In Robert K. Merton's version of strain theory, the set of purposes and interests a culture defines as legitimate objectives for individuals are called _____.

5. Differences in economic and occupational opportunities open to members of different socioeconomic classes are called _____.

6. As proposed by Walter B. Miller, values or focal concerns (toughness, smartness, excitement, fate, and autonomy) of lower-class youths that differ from those of middle-class youths are called _____.

7. In Robert K. Merton's theory, culturally sanctioned methods of attaining individual goals are called _____.

8. Richard A. Cloward and Lloyd E. Ohlin's perspective which holds that gang members turn to delinquency because of a sense of injustice about the lack of legitimate opportunities open to them is called _____.

9. Psychological strategy for dealing with frustrating by becoming hostile towards an unattainable object is called _____.

10. James S. Coleman's perspective which holds that lower-class youth may become delinquent because they lack "social capital," or resources that reside in the social structure, including norms, networks, and relationships are called _____.

11. An approach developed by Shaw, McKay, and others who argue that juvenile delinquency results when social control among the traditional primary groups, such as the family and the neighborhood, breaks down because of social disarray within the community is called

_____.

12. The relatively stable formal and informal arrangements that characterize a society - including its economic arrangements, social institutions, and its values and norms are called

_____.

13. The stress that individuals experience when they cannot attain their goals because of their socioeconomic class is called _____.

14. A theory that proposes that the pressure the social structure exerts on youths who cannot attain cultural success goals will push them to engage in nonconforming behavior is called _____.

Essay:

1. Explain the reasons why social disorganization has been so influential in the development of criminological theory.

2. What are the main criticisms of social disorganization theory as presented by Robert J. Burisk Jr.

3. Explain the six focal concerns of lower-class culture as present by Walter B. Miller.

Multiple Choice:
1. Answer: a   2. Answer: c   3. Answer: b   4. Answer: e   5. Answer: d   6. Answer: c
7. Answer: d   8. Answer: c   9. Answer: c   10. Answer: d   11. Answer: c   12. Answer: e
13. Answer: b   14. Answer: e   15. Answer: a   16. Answer: e   17. Answer: a
18. Answer: c   19. Answer: a   20. Answer: d   21. Answer: b   22. Answer: e
23. Answer: c   24. Answer: b   25. Answer: d

True/False:
1. True   2. False   3. False   4. True   5. False   6. False   7. True   8. False   9. True
10. False

Fill-in-the-blank:
1. blocked opportunity
2. cultural deviance theory
3. cultural transmission theory
4. culturally defined goals
5. differential opportunity structure
6. focal concerns of the lower class
7. institutionalized mans
8. opportunity theory
9. reaction formation
10. social capital theory
11. social disorganization theory
12. social structure
13. status frustration
14. strain theory

WEBSITES

Read the article, *Robert Agnew's Strain Theory Approach,* at
www.justicestudies.com/weblibrary

Read the NIJ publication, *National Evaluation of the "I Have a Dream" Program, at*
www.justicestudies.com/weblibrary

Visit the Project on Human Development in Chicago Neighborhoods (HDNC) Web site via
www.justicestudies.com/webplaces

www.hewett.norfolk.sch.uk

www.criminology.fsu.edu/jjclearinghouse/jj13.html

CHAPTER 5: SOCIAL PROCESS THEORIES

LEARNING OBJECTIVES

After reading this chapter, you should be able to answer the following questions:

1. Do delinquents learn crime from others?

2. Why is it that some young people routinely go from delinquent to non-delinquent acts and then back to delinquent behavior?

3. What control mechanisms insulate teenagers from delinquent behavior?

4. What role does a teen's self concept play in delinquency?

5. Does considering more than one theory increase our ability to explain delinquency?

CHAPTER SUMMARY

Each of the social process theories in this chapter contributes to understanding how adolescents become delinquent. Sutherland's *differential association* theory suggests that individuals learn delinquent behavior from various interactions with antisocial groups. Thus, if they are involved with antisocial groups, they are more likely to accept antisocial conduct norms and definitions. Matza's *drift theory* attempts to explain why juveniles may choose to drift between conventional and delinquent behavior through a process of neutralizing responsibility of their actions. Reckless's *containment theory* states that positive experiences in the home, school and community will lead to good self-concepts and insulate individuals from crime and delinquency. Hirschi's *social control theory* suggests that the more strongly attached adolescents are to various social bonds, the more likely it is they will refrain from becoming involved in delinquent behavior.

Social process theories explain delinquency on the individual level, which is the strength of their analysis. The process of bonding to significant others, drifting in and out of delinquent behavior, and developing strong self-concepts are key conceptual constructs of these theories. Several of these theories suggest a decision-making process by the juvenile.

Although the strength of these theories is found in their mircoanalysis of the behavior and interactions of the individual delinquent, their significant weakness is ignoring the macroanalysis. These theories fail to place adequate emphasis in regard to the impact of political and economic systems on the delinquent. The paradox that emerges between social structural and social process theories is, while one is preoccupied with structural causes, the other fails to include it. Thus, *integrated theory* attempts to combine two or more existing theories to eradicate any deficiencies created by strictly social process and social structural theories. Gottfredson and Hirschi, Elliot, Thornberry, and Hawkins and Weiss, all have contributed significantly to understanding delinquency.

LECTURE OUTLINE

Introduction:
- The story of the Bogle Family.

I. Differential Association Theory
- Sutherland purposes delinquents learn crime from others as part of social interaction.
- Individuals internalize definitions that favor law violations when learning delinquency.
- Learning criminal behavior occurs within intimate personal groups.
- Excess contact with those who favor violations of the law leads to delinquency.
- Differential associations may vary in frequency, duration, priority, and intensity.
- Assumes those who are not delinquent have been socialized to conventional values.
- Difficult to reject the notion of learning and the appeal of the theory is positive.
- Glaser's modification applied the *interactionist* concept of *self* in his theory of *differential identification theory*. Glaser suggests a delinquent identifies themselves with real or imaginary persons who find criminal behavior acceptable.
- Burgess and Aker's *social learning theory* contends that learned behavior comprises the individual's main source of reinforcements and behavior can be imitated or modeled.

A. Evaluation of Differential Association
- Impact of Sutherland's theory on differential identification theory (Glaser) and differential reinforcement theory (Burgess and Akers).
- Critics charge the conceptual terms are vague and does not explain why do some youths do not succumb to delinquency. The delinquent is viewed as a passive vessel with no room for purpose or meaning.

II. Drift Theory and Delinquency
- Delinquency occurs when a juvenile neutralizes himself or herself from the moral bounds.
- The delinquent transiently exists in limbo between convention and crime.
- Delinquency is permissible when responsibility is neutralized; denial of responsibility, denial of injury, denial of victim, condemnation of the condemners, and appeal to higher loyalty.
- Subcultural delinquents are filled with injustice and depend on a memory file of inconsistency.
- Demonstration of valor is related to assertion of a harmful wrong tort instead of crime.
- Not all breaking of the moral bind of law will result in a delinquent act.
- Drift theory can be useful to account for those who commit occasional delinquent acts.

A. Evaluation of Drift Theory
- Drift theory builds on a learning process approach and challenges the notion that delinquents are "constrained" to engage in delinquency.

- J. Hagan integrated drift theory into a life course conceptualization with social control theory.

III. Social Control and Delinquent Behavior
- The core notion of control theory suggests an absence or defective controlling force.
- Delinquency in America: Cyberdelinquents—Bot Herders and Cybercrooks

A. Containment Theory
- Reckless's *containment theory* has two reinforcing elements of inner/outer control.
- Assumes strong *inner* and *outer containment* provides insulation against deviant behavior.
- Inner containment includes; self-control, positive self-image, well-developed superego, high frustration tolerance, high resistance to diversions, high sense of responsibility, ability to find substitute satisfactions, goal orientations and tension-reducing rationalizations.
- Outer containment represents structural buffers which include; norms, goals, expectations, effective supervision/discipline, provision for reasonable activity, opportunity for acceptance, identity, and belongingness.
- Internal *pushes* consists of drives, motives, frustrations, restlessness, disappointments, rebellion, hostility, and feelings of inferiority that encourage a person to engage in unacceptable behavior.
- Societal *pulls* consists of distractions, attractions, temptations, patterns of deviancy, carriers of delinquent patterns, and criminogenic advertising and propaganda in society.
- Reckless theorized if a youth has weak inner and outer containment and the pushes and pulls of society are strong enough, then delinquency is likely to result. Conversely, if the insulation qualities of inner and outer containment are strong enough, then delinquency will likely be diverted.
- Reckless suggests that a "good self-concept" is a precondition of law-abiding behavior.
- Critics charge the concepts are difficult to define and measuring self-concept is questionable.

B. Social Control Theory
- Hirschi's *social control theory* states delinquent acts result when one's bond to society is weak or broken.
- Humans are basically antisocial and naturally capable of committing crime.
- Hirschi suggested people tightly bonded to social groups such as family, the school, and peers are less likely to commit delinquent acts.
- Four main elements; *attachment, commitment, involvement*, and *belief*.
- Attachment includes ties to parents, teachers and friends.
- Commitment includes the degree of commitment to conventional activities such as educational goals, property, and reputation.
- Involvement consists of the amount of time one devotes to conventional activities.
- Belief includes respect for the law and social norms.

C. Evaluation of Social Control Theory
- Provides valuable insights into intrafamily relationships.
- Great amount of empirical data exists to support social control theory.
- Critics charge the questionnaire used by Hirschi to measure delinquency was limited and only measured a few relatively minor acts.
- Social control theory fails to describe the chain of events that weaken social bonds.

IV. Integrated Theories of Delinquency
- Implies the combination of two or more existing theories on the basis of their perceived commonalities.
- Hirschi identified three types; side by side, end to end, up and down integration.
- End to end integration is the most widely used and refers to placing variables in a temporal order so variables of some theories can be operationalized into integrated theory.

A. Issues and Concerns of Integrated Theory
- Concerns of integrated theory include which propositions of a particular theory should be used and some theories tend to explain only certain types of delinquent behavior.
- Additional concerns include generalizations of theories and different assumptions various theories may make in respect to motivations, attitudes and contributing factors to delinquency.

B. Gottfredson and Hirschi's General Theory of Crime
- People who lack self-control will tend to be impulsive, insensitive, physical, risk-taking, shortsighted, and nonverbal, and will tend to engage in criminal acts.
- Self-control is the degree to which an individual is vulnerable to temptation.
- Ineffective or incomplete socialization causes low self-esteem.
- Critics charge a lack of conceptual clarity and key elements remain to be tested.

C. Elliott's Integrated Social Process Theory
- Synthesizes strain, social control, and social learning theory in a single paradigm.
- Contends that living in socially disorganized areas lead youths to develop weak bonds with conventional groups, activities, and norms. Antisocial peer groups provide both positive reinforcement for delinquent behavior and role models for this behavior.
- This theory represents a pure type of integrated theory. Examinations are largely positive.
- Questions have been raised about its power and utility in regard to certain behaviors.

D. Thornberry's Interactional Theory
- Impetus toward delinquency comes from a weakening bond to conventional society.
- Associations with delinquent peers make up the social setting in which delinquency is learned and reinforced.
- The process develops over the person's life cycle.
- Views delinquency as a result of events that occur in the development process.

- Fails to address the presence of middle-class delinquency and ignores race and gender issues.

E. Hawkins and Weis's Social Development Model
- Weis and Hawkins integrate social control and cultural learning theory.
- Developments of attachments to parents will lead to attachments to school and a commitment to education, as well as a belief in conventional behavior and the law.
- Youth not receiving support from families and school are vulnerable to delinquency.
- Interventions that seek to increase the likelihood of social bonding are appropriate.

V. Social Process and Delinquency Across the Life Course

A. Lack of Competence in Adolescence
- Competence and social influence at the end of adolescence shapes evolving life course.
- Choice of attractive opportunities permits the most competent to take advantages.

B. Cumulative Disadvantages
- Personal deficits lead to cumulative disadvantages.
- Each negative event in life tends to limit the positive options available to some people.

C. Turning Point
- Sampson and Laub found four turning points in the desistance process (marriage, reform school, military, and neighborhood change).
- Desistance requires positive attitudes, prosocial behaviors, and reinforcing transitions.

KEY TERMS

commitment to delinquency   David Matza's term for the attachment that juvenile may have to delinquent identify and values.

commitment to social bond   The attachment that a juvenile has to conventional institutions and activities.

containment theory   Walter C. Reckless's theory that contends that strong inner and outer containment provide an insulation against the pushes and pulls of delinquent behavior in society.

control theory   This theory suggests humans must be controlled to repress delinquent tendencies.

differential association theory   Sutherland's theory that suggests that individuals internalize definitions that favor violating the law to a higher degree, than definitions that favor law abiding behaviors.

differential identification theory   Daniel Glaser's modification of differential association that applied the interactionist concept of self.

drift theory   Matza's theory which contends juveniles may drift from conventional to criminal behavior when neutralizing themselves from the moral bounds of the law.

neutralization theory   This theory suggests youngsters justify their actions by neutralizing responsibility through denial of responsibility, injury, and victim, and condemnation of the condemners, and by appealing to a higher loyalty.

social control theory   Theory that criminal behavior is controlled by the social bond or processes of socialization, in which delinquent acts will likely occur when an individual's bond to society is weak or broken.

social development model   Theory that integrates two or more existing theories on the basis of perceived commonalities. Includes side-to-side, end-to-end, and up and down integrations.

social process theories   Theories of delinquency that examine the interactions between individuals and their environments that influence them to become involved in delinquency.

soft determinism   David Matza's view that delinquents are neither wholly free or constrained but somewhere in between.

Practice Test

Multiple Choice

1. The story of the Bogel family illustrates _____.
a. mental illness creates a fertile ground for crime
b. race affects crime rates
c. how criminal behavior came be passed from one generation to the next
d. how income is the main predictor of criminal activity
e. geographic regions have different crime rates

2. Edwin Sutherland formulated the theory of _____.
a. broken windows
b. differential association
c. differential opportunity
d. anomie
e. containment theory

3. One of the basic premises of differential association is that criminal behavior is a product of
_____.
a. biology
b. genetics
c. psychological problems
d. poverty
e. social interaction

4. Edwin Sutherland first developed his theory in his text _____.
a. *Thinking About Crime*
b. *The Meaning of Crime*
c. *Introduction to Criminal Justice*
d. *Principles of Criminology*
e. *The Criminal Mind*

5. The first principle of differential association is that "Criminal behavior is _____".
a. learned
b. hereditary
c. genetic
d. based on income
e. based on education

6. The author of *Delinquency and Drift* is _____.
a. Edwin Sutherland
b. Albert Cohen
c. Rachel Shaw
d. James Q. Wilson
e. David Matza

7. The theory which contends juveniles may drift from conventional to criminal behavior when neutralizing themselves from the moral bounds of the law is called _____.
a. drift theory
b. differential association
c. delinquency and opportunity
d. gang theory
e. conflict theory

8. Which of the following is *not* one of the 5 techniques of neutralization?
a. denial of responsibility
b. denial of injury
c. denial of conviction
d. condemnation of the condemners
e. denial of knowledge

9. The authors of neutralization theory are _____?
a. Richard Cloward and Lloyd Ohlin
b. Gresham M. Sykes and David Matza
c. Rachel Shaw and Amanda Miller
d. Travis Hirschi and Michael Gottfredson
e. Joseph G. Weis and J. David Hawkins

10. Control theorists agree on one especially significant point: _____.
a. all crime has a biological base
b. human beings must be held in check, or controlled
c. all crime has a psychological base
d. long prison sentences greatly reduce crime
e. crime has a sociological basics

11. Containment theory was developed by _____.
a. Karl Marx
b. Edwin Sutherland
c. Edwin Schur
d. Walter C. Reckless
e. Albert Cohen

12. Jeanson James Ancheta is famous for _____?
a. armed bank robberies
b. selling cocaine
c. internet hacking
d. serial murder
e. political bribes

13. Reckless and Dinitz concluded from these studies that one of the preconditions of law-abiding conduct is a good _____.
a. income
b. family structure
c. grade point level
d. relationship with siblings
e. self-concept

14. The theorist who is most closely identified with social control theory is _____?
a. Travis Hirschi
b. Thomas Hobbs
c. Max Weber
d. Emile Durkheim
e. Edwin Sutherland

15. Another name for social control theory is _____.
a. differential association
b. bonding
c. conflict theory
d. societal reaction theory
e. drift theory

16. Which of the following writers believed that humans are basically antisocial and sinful?
a. Thomas Hobbs
b. Puritan theologians
c. Sigmund Freud
d. all of the above

17. Travis Hirschi calls "the tendency or propensity of the individual to seek short-term immediate pleasure which provides money without work, sex without courtship, revenge without court delays" _____.
a. crime
b. deviance
c. a violation of the moral code
d. misbehavior
e. misconduct

18. Who wrote *A General Theory of Crime*?
a. Richard Cloward and Lloyd Ohlin
b. Gresham M. Sykes and David Matza
c. Rachel Shaw and Amanda Miller
d. Travis Hirschi and Michael Gottfredson
e. Joseph G. Weis and J. David Hawkins

19. John Claussen's classic study of children found that _____.
a. income determined if a child would become a violent criminal
b. children need psychological counseling if they are to avoid criminal behavior
c. competence and social influence at the end of adolescence gave shape to the evolving life course
d. a parent's educational level determined the child's likelihood of committing a crime

20. David Matza's term for the attachment that juvenile may have to delinquent identify and values is called _____.
a. containment theory
b. commitment to delinquency
c. control theory
d. commitment to social bond

21. The attachment that a juvenile has to conventional institutions and activities is called_____.
a. containment theory
b. commitment to delinquency
c. control theory
d. commitment to social bond

22. Walter C. Reckless's theory that contends that strong inner and outer containment provide an insulation against the pushes and pulls of delinquent behavior in a society is called

_____.
a. containment theory
b. commitment to delinquency
c. control theory
d. commitment to social bond

23. The theory that suggests humans must be controlled to repress delinquent tendencies is called _____.
a. containment theory
b. commitment to delinquency
c. control theory
d. commitment to social bond

24. Sutherland's theory that suggests that individuals internalize definitions that favor violating the law to a higher degree than definitions that favor law abiding behaviors is called

_____.
a. anomie theory
b. containment theory
c. control theory
d. drift theory
e. differential association theory

25. David Matza's view that delinquents are neither wholly free or constrained but somewhere in between is called _____.
a. hard determinism
b. classical determinism
c. biological determinism
d. soft determinism

True/False:

1. Differential Association was first coined by the famous sociologist Albert Cohen.

2. Drift, according to Matza, means that "the delinquency transiently exists in limbo between convention and crime, responding in turn to the demands of each, flirting now with one, now the other, but postponing commitment, evading decision.

3. Reckless and Dinitz concluded from these studies that one of the preconditions of law-abiding conduct is a good appearance.

4. Travis Hirschi argued that an attachment to peers would reduce the teenagers attachment to parents.

5. Hirschi found that the more a boy was involved in school and leisure activities, the less likely he was to become involved in delinquency.

6. According to your authors, although social control theory cannot explain all acts of delinquency, it still has more empirical today than any other explanation of delinquency.

7. According to Gottfredson and Hirschi ineffective or incomplete socialization causes low self-control.

8. When self-control is formed in childhood, quite often it has to be reformed in adolescence and then again in adulthood.

9. In Michael Gottfredson's interactional theory of delinquency the initial impetus toward delinquency comes from a weakening of the person's bond to conventional society, represented by attachment to parents, commitment to school and the belief in conventional values.

10. The author of differential association is David Matza.

Fill-in-the-blank:

1. David Matza's term for the attachment that a delinquent juvenile has to a deviant identity and value is called _____.

2. In Travis Hirschi's theory of social control, the attachment that a juvenile has to conventional institutions and activities is called _____.

3. Walter C. Reckless's theoretical perspective that strong inner containment and reinforcing external containment provide insulation against delinquent and criminal behavior is called

_____.

4. Any of several theoretical approaches that maintain human beings must be held in check, or somehow be controlled, if delinquent tendencies are to be repressed are called

_____.

5. Edward H. Sutherland's view that delinquency is learned from others; and that delinquent behavior is t be expected of individuals who have internalized a preponderance of definitions that are favorable to law violations is called _____.

6. A modification of differential association theory offered by Daniel Glaser is called

_____.

7. David Matza's theoretical perspective that juveniles neutralize the moral hold of society and drift into delinquent behavior is called _____.

8. Gresham M. Sykes and David Matza's theory examining how youngsters attempt to justify or rationalize their responsibility for delinquent acts is called _____.

9. A perspective advocated by Travis Hirschi and others, who propose that delinquent acts result when a juvenile's bond to society is weak or broken is called _____.

10. A perspective based on the integration of social control and cultural learning theories which proposes the development of attachments to parents will lead to attachments to school and a commitment to education as well as a belief in and commitment to conventional behavior and the law is called _____.

11. Theoretical approaches to delinquency that examine the interactions between individuals and their environments, especially those that might influence them to become involved in delinquent behavior are called _____.

12. David Matza claimed that the concept of soft determinism offers the best resolution of the debate between advocates of free will and positivists. Matza's view is that delinquents are neither wholly free nor wholly constrained in their choice of actions is referred to as

_____.

Essay:

1. List the 9 propositions of Differential Association.

2. Explain the 5 Techniques of Neutralization.

3. According to Hirschi, Containment Theory is made-up of 4 main elements. Explain each of these elements.

4. Explain the concept of Drift Theory.

5. Explain the criminal career of Jeanson James Ancheta.

6. Explain Gottfredson's and Hirschi's general theory of crime.

Multiple Choice:
1. Answer: a   2. Answer: b   3. Answer: e   4. Answer: d   5. Answer: a   6. Answer: d
7. Answer: a   8. Answer: e   9. Answer: b   10. Answer: b   11. Answer: d   12. Answer: c
13. Answer: e   14. Answer: a   15. Answer: b   16. Answer: d   17. Answer: a
18. Answer: d   19. Answer: c   20. Answer: b   21. Answer: d   22. Answer: a
23. Answer: c   24. Answer: e   25. Answer: d

True/False:
1. False   2. True   3. False   4. False   5. True   6. True   7. True   8. False   9. False
10. False

Fill-in-the-blank:
1. commitment to delinquency
2. commitment to the social bond
3. containment theory
4. control theory
5. differential association theory
6. differential identification theory
7. drift theory
8. neutralization theory
9. social control theory
10. social development model
11. social process theories
12. soft determinism

WEBSITES

Read the NIJ-sponsored research publication, *Trajectories of Violent Offending and risk Status in Adolescence and Early Adulthood,* at www.justicestudies.com/weblibrary

Read the article, *Social Learning and Structural Factors in Adolescent Substance Use,* at www.justicestudies.com/weblibrary

Read the OJJDP publication, *Causes and Correlates: Findings nad Implications,* at www.justicestudies.com/weblibrary

Read the testimony of Mr. John Wilson, Acting Administrator of the Office of Juvenile Justice and Delinquency Prevention, before the U.S. House of Representatives, Committee on the Judiciary on October 2, 2000, at www.justicestudies.com/weblibrary

Read the OJJDP Fact Sheet, *Highlights of Findings from the Denver Youth Survey,* at www.justicestudies.com/weblibrary

Visit the Serious, Violent, and/or Habitual Offenders section of the Juvenile Justice Evaluation Center's Web site via www.justicestudies.com/webplaces

Visit the National Youth Violence Prevention Resource Center's Web site via www.justicestudies.com/weblibrary

www.criminolgy.fsu.edu/crimtheory/sutherland.html

http://www.cnn.com/SPECIALS/1998/schools/

CHAPTER 6: SOCIAL INTERACTIONIST THEORIES OF DELINQUENCY

LEARNING OBJECTIVES

After reading this chapter you should be able to answer the following questions:

1. How important is the concept of labeling as a cause of future behavior?

2. What kinds of youngsters become more determined to succeed because they have been labeled?

3. Does peer evaluation affect some young people more than others?

4. How does social class affect the system's response to a troublesome youth?

CHAPTER SUMMARY

This chapter examines three explanations used to understand juvenile delinquency. Social reaction is the key concept used to evaluate *labeling* and *symbolic interactionist theories* of delinquency, and the *conflict approach* to delinquency. All three of these theories focus on the role that social and economic groups, and institutions have in producing delinquent behavior.

Social reaction takes place in a particular context that will vary within certain individuals, and groups, such as family, groups, school settings, the justice system and society's political decision makers. Social reaction also takes place during the process of interaction. The process will vary from the formation of the social self, to how one responds to given labels for what is perceived as unacceptable behavior, and to the reaction of what is interpreted as economic exploitation by the larger society. Oppression is instrumental when evaluating what takes place during the labeling process and to understanding exploitation of the lower-class youth.

Variations in conflict theory include the dimensions of *socioeconomic, power* and *authority*, and *group* and *cultural conflict*. Marxist theorists relate delinquency to issues of alienation and powerlessness among lower-class youth. The dominant classes, in an attempt to control the subordinate groups, create definitions of delinquency traditionally for economic gain. Thus, the lack of social justice in America becomes a constant class struggle and conflict approach between upper and lower classes. Weber discussed social stratification in terms of "life chances" and argued that they were differentially related to social class. From this perspective, delinquency is a result of political struggles among different groups attempting to promote or enhance their own life chances. Sellins defined conflict as a result of divergent rules of conduct for a specific life situation that conflicts with opposing *conduct norms* held by other groups or individuals. Thus, the more complex a culture becomes, the more likely it is that the number of normative groups, which affect a person, will be large. *Peacemaking* criminologists argue that we need to deescalate violence through conciliation, mediation and dispute settlement.

- Weber discussed *"life chances"* are differentially related to social class.
- Turk constructed an analysis based on conflict and domination between authorities and subjects. Authorities create, interpret, and enforce right-wrong standards.
- Hagen linked power and control to gender and nonserious delinquency suggesting that the greater control of girls explains why boys are frequently more delinquent.
- Regoli and Hewitt's theory of *differential oppression* based on authority is unjustly used against children. Theory employs biological ideas, sociological and psychological theories about behavior: (1) children are easy targets for adults due to size differences, (2) oppression of children falls along a continuum of benign to malignant abuse, 3) oppression leads to adaptive reactions by children, and 4) children's adaptations to oppression create and reinforce the view of children as inferior subordinate beings.
- Sellins and Vold advocated conflict criminology from *group and cultural perspective.*
- Sellins discussed *"conduct norms"* as the ways members of a group should act meaning the more complex a culture becomes, the more likely the number of normative groups will affect a person's behavior.
- Sellins also developed *primary* and *secondary culture conflict* concepts.
- Vold states, as groups move into each others territory competition is inevitable and results in a winner and loser unless compromise is reached. Minority groups are at odds with police maintained by society.
- Delinquency International: Juvenile Crime Rises in Russia

B. Marxist Criminology and Explanations of Delinquent Behavior
- *Alienation* and *powerlessness* among youth who remain in holding until they enter the workforce.
- Limited voting power, lack of organized lobbies, and hold few positions of power.
- Quinney stated violent gang activity might be a collective response of adolescents.
- Marxists purport lengthening of the rites of passage contributes to alienation of youths.
- Certain acts are termed delinquent because it is in the interest of the ruling class.
- *"Haves"* exploit the *"have-nots"* and children become a marginal class.
- *Instrumental theory* suggests that status is relative to delinquency.
- Social injustice linked to; poor youth, sexist treatment of female offenders, and racism.
- Chambliss and *"The Saints and the Roughnecks"* study suggests inequality in justice.

C. Alienation and Delinquency
- Structural and integrated Marxist theory contends that power relations subjected to most lower-class workers are coercive (Colvin).
- Juveniles are alienated from parental bonds and likely to be placed in coercive school control situations.

D. Evaluation of Conflict Theory
- All call attention to nation's macrostructural flaws.
- Radical humanism is rooted in structural inequalities of the social order.

KEY TERMS

capitalism   An economic system of private capital that are determined by private decision, prices, production, and the distribution of goods that are determined by competition in a free market.

conduct norms   Description for rules of a group in regard to how its members should act.

conflict theory   Theory that delinquency is explained by socioeconomic class, power and authority relationships, and by group and cultural differences.

cultural conflict   Sellins's perspective that suggests delinquency or crime arises because of conflicts that individuals experience as member of a subculture that has its own particular conduct norms that differ from the dominant groups.

instrumental Marxists   Group members who view the entire apparatus of crime control as the tool or instrument of the ruling class.

instrumental theory   Schwendinger's theory that states the most important variable in identifying delinquency potential for adolescents is their relative status position among other adolescents.

labeling perspective   Assumes society creates deviance by negatively labeling those who are apprehended as different from others, and any subsequent interactions are influenced by the meaning and perception derived from the label.

Marxist criminology   View that crime and delinquency in capitalist society emerges due to the efforts of the powerful to maintain their power at all costs.

power control thesis   John Hagan and colleagues view the relationship between gender and delinquency as being linked to power and control.

primary deviation   Lemert's theoretical concept that deviance committed in the initial act leads to a negative reaction by the social audience and may lead to the attaching of a negative label.

process of becoming delinquent   Lemert's labeling theory contends the process of acquiring a delinquent identity occurs through a sequence of interaction leading to secondary deviation.

Radical criminology   A perspective that holds that the causes of crime are rooted in social conditions that empower the wealthy and the politically well organized but disenfranchise the less fortunate.

radical nonintervention   Schur's purposed policy of delinquency, which advised authorities to not intervene whenever possible.

secondary deviation   Lemert's theoretical concept that deviance committed in the initial act leads to a negative reaction by the social audience and may lead to the attaching of a negative label.

social reaction theories   Theories that focus on the role that social and economic groups and institutions have on producing delinquent behavior.

symbolic interactionist theory   Theory in social psychology that stresses the process of interaction among human beings at the symbolic level.

theory of differential oppression   Regoli and Hewitt's theory based on combinations of biological ideas, and sociological and psychological theories that authority is unjustly used against children.

Practice Test

Multiple Choice:

1. The vignette at the beginning of the chapter involved a crime committed against _____.
a. Tom Cruise
b. Taren Burris
c. President George Bush Sr.
d. President Bill Clinton
e. Michael Jordan

2. The _____ assumes society creates deviance by negatively labeling those who are apprehended as different from others, and any subsequent interactions are influenced by the meaning and perception derived from the label.
a. conflict theory
b. economic theory
c. heredity theory
d. labeling perspective
e. feeble-mindedness theory

3. The earliest formulation of labeling theory was developed by _____.
a. Robert Merton
b. Walter B. Miller
c. Edwin Sutherland
d. Frank Tannenbaum
e. Frederick M. Thrasher

4. "The process of making the criminal, therefore, is a process of tagging, defining, identifying, segregating, describing, emphasizing, making conscious and self-conscious; it becomes a way of stimulating, suggesting, emphasizing, and evoking the very traits that are complained of", was written by _____.
a. Robert Merton
b. Walter B. Miller
c. Edwin Sutherland
d. Frank Tannenbaum
e. Frederick M. Thrasher

5. Who's name was most associated with the term "dramatization of evil" _____.
a. Robert Merton
b. Walter B. Miller
c. Edwin Sutherland
d. Frank Tannenbaum
e. Frederick M. Thrasher

6. What author made popular the term "primary and secondary deviation"?
a. Edwin H. Lemert
b. Robert Merton
c. Walter B. Miller
d. Frederick M. Thrasher
e. Frank Tannenbaum

7.   Lemert's theoretical concept that deviance committed in the initial act leads to a negative reaction by the social audience and may lead to the attaching of a negative label was called

_____.
a. first deviation
b. main deviation
c. primary deviation
d. temporary deviation
e. beginning deviation

8. Under Lemert, the response of society to deviant behavior is associated with the term

_____.
a. primary deviation
b. secondary deviation
c. main deviation
d. beginning deviation
e. first deviation

9. Who wrote that " social groups create deviance by making the rules who's infraction constitutes deviance…."?
a. Edwin H. Lempert
b. Howard Becker
c. Walter B. Miller
d. Edwin Schur
e. Frank Tannenbaum

10. Which of the following authors would be most associated with the sentence " Leave the kids alone whenever possible"?
a. Edwin H. Lempert
b. Howard Becker
c. Walter B. Miller
d. Edwin Schur
e. Frank Tannenbaum

11. "Kansas Charlie" was charged with _____ when he was 15 years old.
a. selling drugs
b. performing prostitution
c. murdering two boys
d. committing an armed robbery
e. stealing a bicycle

12. The central medium through which symbolic interaction occurs is _____.
a. language
b. financial advantage
c. education
d. race
e. sex

13. Projecting one's self into the role of other persons and appraising, from their stand point, the situation is called _____.
a. acting
b. role taking
c. analyzing
d. calculating
e. hypothesizing

14. The concept of "looking-glass self" was originated by _____.
a. Edwin H. Lempert
b. Howard Becker
c. Walter B. Miller
d. Charles H. Cooley
e. Frank Tannenbaum

15. The concept of "self as an object" is best related to _____.
a. Edwin H. Lempert
b. Howard Becker
c. Walter B. Miller
d. Edwin Schur
e. George H. Mead

16. The development of the conflict model is indebted to the concept of _____.
a. education
b. sociobiology theories
c. dialectics
d. equality
e. none of the above

17. A prevailing idea, or "thesis", according to Hegel, would eventually be challenged by an opposing idea, or "antithesis". This is called _____.
a. positivism
b. sociobiology theories
c. dialectics
d. hypothesizing
e. the scientific method

18. What type of theorists view laws as tools created by the powerful for their own benefit?
a. symbolic interactionists
b. conflict
c. functionalists
d. social biologists
e. anthropologists

19. Karl Marx saw the history of all societies as the history of _____.
a. class struggles
b. changing technologies
c. changing philosophies
d. evolution
e. social biology

20. Who is the author of *The Communist Manifesto*?
a. Edwin H. Lempert
b. Karl Marx
c. Walter B. Miller
d. Edwin Schur
e. George H. Mead

21. The rules for a group in regard to how its members should act are called _____.
a. laws
b. regulations
c. behavior patterns
d. conduct norms
e. society expectations

22. According to Thorsten Sellin, _____ occurs when an individual or group comes into contact with an individual or group from another culture and the conduct norms of the two cultures are not compatible.
a. primary deviance
b. secondary deviance
c. primary culture conflict
d. secondary culture conflict
e. none of the above

23. According to Thorsten Sellin, _____ refers to the conflict arising whenever society has diverging subcultures with conduct norms.
a. primary deviance
b. secondary deviance
c. primary culture conflict
d. secondary culture conflict
e. none of the above

24. Marxist criminologists argue that certain acts are termed delinquent because _____.
a. those acts are dangerous and harm all of society
b. everyone agrees that those acts should not be allowed
c. it is in the interest of the ruling class to so define them
d. it is in the interest of the lower class to so define them

25. Who is the author of *The Child Savers*?
a. Karl Marx
b. Robert Merton
c. Emile Durkheim
d. Max Weber
e. Anthony Platt

True/False:

1. Labeling theory is based on the premise that society creates deviance by labeling those who are apprehended as different from other individuals.

2. The central medium through which symbolic interaction occurs is economic advantage.

3. George Herbert Mead's analysis of the social act is the basis of most versions of contemporary symbolic interactionism.

4. The important mechanism by which interactants influence each other is role taking, which Mead viewed as the key to social control.

5. Emile Durkheim, a twentieth-century conflict theorist, argued that unity and discord are inextricably intertwined and together act as an integrative force in society.

6. Robert Merton proposed that social researchers would be wise to opt for the conflict model because of its more realistic view that society is held together by constraint rather than consensus, not by universal agreement but by the coercion of some people by others.

7. Karl Marx, the originator of conflict theory, wrote extensively on the issue of crime.

8. Richard Quinney has argued that the criminal law is a social control instrument of the state.

9. In Moscow, more minors are breaking the law and their crimes are growing crueler.

10. Marxists criminologists contend that the dominant classes create definitions of crime to oppress the subordinate classes, that the economic system exploits lover-class youth, and that social justice is lacking for lower-class youth.

Fill-in-the-blank:

1. An economic system in which private individuals or corporations own and control capital (wealth and means of production) and in which competitive free markets control prices, production, and the distribution of goods is called _____.

2. The rules of a group governing the way its members should act under particular conditions and the violation of these rules that arouses a group reaction is called _____.

3. A perspective which holds that delinquency can be explained by socioeconomic class, by power and authority relationships, and by group and cultural differences is called _____.

4. Social scientific thinkers who combine Marxist theory with the insights of later theorists, such as Sigmund Freud are called _____.

5. A perspective proposed by Thorsten Sellin and others which includes the idea that delinquency or crime arises because individuals are members of a subculture who have conduct norms which are in conflict with those of the wider society is called _____.

6. A group whose members view the entire apparatus of crime control as a tool or instrument of the ruling class is called _____.

7. A perspective developed by Herman Schwendinger and Julia Siegel Schwendinger, which holds that the most important t variable predicting delinquency in teenagers is their status position relative to that of their peers is called _____.

8. The view that society creates the delinquent by labeling those who are apprehended as "different" from other youth, when in reality they are different primarily because they have been "tagged" with a deviant label is called _____.

9. The view of John Hagan and his associates that the relationship between gender and delinquency is linked to issues of power and control is called _____.

10. According to labeling theory, the initial act of deviance that causes a person to be labeled a deviant is called _____.

11. In labeling theory, the concept that the process of acquiring a delinquent identity takes place in a number of steps is called _____.

12. A perspective which holds the causes of crime are rooted in social conditions that empower the wealthy and the politically well organized but disenfranchise the less fortunate is called

_____.

13. Edwin Schur's proposed policy toward delinquents, which advises that authorities should "leave the kids alone whenever possible" is called _____.

14. According to the labeling theory, deviance that is a consequence of societal reaction to an initial delinquent act is called _____.

15. According to many conflict-oriented criminologists, unfairness in the juvenile justice system resulting from the fact that poor youth tend to be disproportionately represented, female status offenders are subjected to sexist treatment, and racial minorities are dealt with more harshly than whites is called

_____.

16. Theoretical perspectives that derive their explanatory power from the give and take that continuously occurs between social groups, or between individuals and society are called _____.

Answer: social interactionist theories

17. A group that argues the form taken by the legal system in a society can work to reinforce capitalist social relations is called _____.

Answer: structural Marxists

18. A perspective in social psychology that analyzes the process of interaction among human beings at the symbolic level, and which influences the development of several social process theories of delinquent behavior is called _____.

Answer: symbolic interactionist theory

19. Robert M Regoli and John D. Hewitt's view that in the United States authority is unjustly used against children, who must adapt to adults' ideas of what constitutes "good children" is called

_____.

Answer: theory of differential oppression

Essay:

1. Explain the concept of primary and secondary deviation.

2. Explain the concept of labeling theory and "The Dramatization of Evil".

3. What are the strengths of labeling theory?

4. The theory of differential oppression is organized around 4 principles. What are those 4 principles?

5. Explain the term "dramatization of evil". What does it mean and how does it create delinquency?

Multiple Choice:
1. Answer: c   2. Answer: d   3. Answer: d   4. Answer: d   5. Answer: d   6. Answer: a
7. Answer: c   8. Answer: b   9. Answer: b   10. Answer: d   11. Answer: c   12. Answer: a
13. Answer: b   14. Answer: d   15. Answer: e   16. Answer: c   17. Answer: c
18. Answer: b   19. Answer: a   20. Answer: b   21. Answer: d   22. Answer: c
23. Answer: d   24. Answer: c   25. Answer: e

True/False:
1. True   2. False   3. True   4. True   5. False   6. False   7. False   8. True   9. True
10. True

Fill-in-the-blank:
1. capitalism
2. conduct norms
3. conflict theory
4. critical criminologists
5. culture conflict theory
6. instrumentalist Marxists
7. instrumental theory
8. labeling theory
9. power-control thesis
10. primary deviation
11. process of becoming deviant
12. radical criminology
13. radical nonintervention
14. secondary deviation
15. social injustice
16. social interactionist theories
17. structural Marxists
18. symbolic interactionist theory
19. theory of differential oppression

WEBSITES

Read the OJJDP publication, *Report of the Comprehensive Strategy task Force on Serious, Violent and Chronic Juvenile Offenders – Part 1,* at www.justicestudies.com/weblibrary

Read the OJJDP publication, *Report of the Comprehensive strategy Task Force on Serious, Violent, Chronic Juvenile Offenders – Part 2,* at www.justicestudies.com/weblibrary

Learn about OJJDP's Juvenile Mentoring Program (JUMP) at www.justicestudies.com/weblibrary

Learn about labeling theory from CrimeTheory.com via www.justicestudies.com/webplaces

www.criminolgy.fsu.edu/crimtheory/becker.htm

www.capitalism.org

CHAPTER 7: GENDER AND DELINQUENCY

LEARNING OBJECTIVES

After you read this chapter, you should be able to answer the following questions:

1. How is gender important to an understanding of delinquency?

2. How are the categories of gender, class, and race helpful in understanding the issues faced by female delinquent and status offenders?

3. What strides towards gender equality have been made in the past few years? What led to these changes?

CHAPTER SUMMARY

This chapter examines the nature of female delinquency. *Feminist theory* purports that females are positioned in society to become victimized by their male counterparts. Females situated in a patriarchal society, appear to be controlled in greater amounts at home, school, and in the community. The acceptance and rejection of their expected social norms is explored from a contextual analysis.

The basic notion among feminists and nonfeminists is that delinquency theories are preoccupied with why males commit delinquent acts. Some feminists suggest that separate theories are needed to explain female delinquency, while others disagree saying that existing theories are adequate to explain female and male delinquency alike. Considerable evidence supports that female delinquency operates through the same sociological factors as male delinquency. This position also infers that reductionism occurs by assuming women are universal and distinct from men in their delinquency. However, certain evidence exists that suggests new approaches are needed to examine the multiple marginality of adolescent females. Criminologists have generally ignored problems of oppression through sexism, racism, and class, and feminists attempted to examine the relationship of these factors to female delinquency.

Female delinquency studies reveal females receive harsher treatment than males by the juvenile justice system. Some evidence shows that girls are treated punitively for status offenses. However, they receive the benefits of chivalry when committing delinquent offenses. Little evidence supports that female delinquency is more abnormal and pathological than male delinquency. Additionally, the *women's liberation movement* has not been instrumental in influencing delinquency as once speculated by some researchers.

LECTURE OUTLINE

Introduction
- Meda Chesney-Lind claims the study of delinquency is gender biased toward males.
- Females are more controlled than males, they enjoy more social support, and are less disposed to commit crime with fewer opportunities.
- Chesney-Lind suggests a need for a *feminist model of delinquency.*
- The case of Noemi and her sister.

I. Gender and Delinquency
- Gender is a social construction in which children are socialized into gender arrangements.
- Girls are more focused on relationships than boys and tend to have more negative body images.
- Disruptions in family, community, and school affect females more negatively than males.
- Abuses within the juvenile system include; foul/demanding language by staff, inappropriate touching, pushing and hitting by staff, placement in isolation, deprivation of clean clothing.
- Two-thirds of the females in the juvenile justice system are minorities.
- Few gender specific programs (need for intensive family-based programs)

II. Gender Neutral Perspectives on Explanations of Female Delinquency
- Biological and psychological explanations view adolescent females through *sexism.*
- Some criminologists challenge the need for distinct and separate theories.

A. Biological and Constitutional Explanations
- Lombroso: women are primitive, less intelligent, unable to feel pain, lack moral refinement, passive, and predisposed to live dull/unimaginative lives. Women criminals inherit male characteristic, excessive body hair, moles, wrinkles, crow's feet, and abnormal craniums.
- Cowie noted physical overdevelopment results in sexual promiscuity and menstruation is a reminder females will never be males.

B. Psychological Explanations
- Thomas suggests females are *anabolic* (motionless, lethargic, and conservative). He argues girls are driven by four wishes; (1) desire for new experience, (2) desire for security, (3) desire for response, and (4) desire for recognition. Thomas suggested prostitution was a result of the girl's need for love, recognition and ambition.
- Freud suggested that women's sex organs make them inferior to men. Mothers replace the "lost penis" with a baby, and her drive of accomplishment is her longing for a "penis." He also suggested they have little social sense.
- Pollak suggested the crimes of women largely go unreported or are hidden. Women are inherently deceitful.
- The *chivalry factor* is advanced as root cause of hidden crime. Pollak also suggests that early development is related to immoral/delinquent behavior.
- Psychologists suggest a relationship between psychological impairment and delinquency such as sexual abuse and prostitution are due to poor self-esteem.

- Sexism thrives in psychological theories as in the biological explanations.

C. Sociological Explanations
- Datesman found the perception of limited opportunity is more related to female delinquency than male delinquency.
- *Blocked opportunity theory* is more predictive than other variables, however the notion is more applicable to whites than nonwhites.
- Adler argues the rise in female delinquency is related to *women's liberation movement*. Females become more competitive and aggressive.
- Critics charge that minority women were not part of the liberation movement, and changes began prior to the movement. Weis contends female criminality is more of a social invention.
- Hirschi's *social control theory* contends sex-role socialization is greater for females and they are supervised more closely by parents.
- The general theory of crime (GTC) contends females have more self-contol and less access to delinquency compared to males.
- Differential association theory suggests boys are more impacted by differential associations than females.
- The *masculinity hypothesis* purports as females become more male-like they become more delinquent.
- Peer group influence observes that females are more likely to be delinquent in mixed-sex groups.
- Hagan's *power control theory* suggests when daughters are freed from patriarchal influence they are more likely to become delinquent.
- *Labeling* and *interactionist theory* suggest that delinquency is determined in part by the self as conceived by symbolic interactions, which in turn is determined by the process of labeling by significant others. Parents are more likely to falsely accuse male delinquents.

D. Evaluating Explanations of Delinquency
- *Gender* is a strong correlate of delinquency. Biological theories are the least predictive. Personal maladjustment is overemphasized as well.
- Some feminists are satisfied that sociological studies conclude males and females are differentially exposed by the same criminogenic factors.

III. Types of Feminist Theories
- Five expressions; liberal, phenomenological, socialist, Marxist, and radical feminism.

A. Liberal Feminism
- Theory calls for women's equality of opportunity and freedom choice.
- Seeks to *androgynize* gender roles and eliminate discriminatory practices.
- Suggests delinquent women imitate males.

B. Phenomenological Feminism
- Concerned with the impact of chivalrous treatment for female offenders

- Some suggest females have been treated more harshly than males by the justice system.

C. Socialist Feminism
- Views class and gender relations as equal in the interactions with each other.
- Low female crime rates correlated to women's powerless position in society.

D. Marxist Feminism
- Males dominate the private property structure in society.
- Sexism is a result of capitalist relations that structure women, juvenile power and crime.

E. Radical Feminism
- Masculine power is the root cause of all social relations and inequality.
- Focus on sexual violence directed toward women.

IV. A Feminist Theory of Delinquency
- An expression of radical feminism contends that girl's victimization and relationship to crime has been systematically ignored. Chesney-Lind suggests that girls are often in juvenile court at the insistence of their parents.
- Chesney-Lind proposed; (1) girls are frequently victims of violence and sexual abuse, (2) their victimizers have the ability to invoke official agencies of social control, (3) as girls runaway from oppressive environments, they are perceived as escaped convicts, and (4) it is not by accident that impoverished girls become involved in criminal activities.
- Third-Wave Feminism

V. Gender Bias and the Processing of Female Delinquents

A. Gender Relations
- Females tend to receive discriminatory treatment by agents of the system.
- Female status offenders are more likely to be referred to authorities than males. Younger females receive harsher punishment than older females. Police tend to act paternalistic with young female offenders.
- Adolescent girls engaged in sexual activity are more likely to be placed into confinement.
- Females are commonly confined longer than males for technical probation violations.
- On balance, the *Juvenile Justice and Delinquency Prevention Act of 1974*, may be preventing some discrimination of female status offenders.

B. The Influence of Class
- Problems of adolescence related to poverty sets the stage for homelessness, unemployment, drug use, survival sex, and other more serious delinquent acts.
- Lower-class females are more likely to have unsatisfactory experiences at school, be victims of sexual abuse, deal with pregnancy and motherhood issues, and be involved in drugs/alcohol.

C. Racial Discrimination
- Racism and poverty go hand-in-hand. Coping with same type of problems; abuse, drugs, violence and gang membership.
- Girls of color receive less chivalry then middle-class white girls.
- Minority girls are viewed as more dangerous to society than whites.

D. The Total is Greater Than The Sum Of Its Parts
- *Multiple oppression* which suggests that gender, class and race are interlocking forms of oppression and the whole is greater than the parts.

VI. Gender Across The Life Course
- Females are more likely to desist from crime faster than males due to conventional life patterns such as marriage, parenting, and work.
- Chronic offending appears to be lower for females compared to males.

KEY TERMS

chivalry factor   Purports that males treat offending females more leniently due to their gender.

feminist theory of delinquency   Expression of radical feminism which contends that girl's victimization and the relationship between the experience and girl's crime have been systematically ignored.

gender   The culturally defined ways of acting as a male or a female that become part of an individual's personal sense of self.

gender roles   societal expectations of what is masculine and what is feminine behavior.

masculinity hypothesis   Proposition in which girls become more boy-like and acquire more masculine traits as they become more delinquent.

peer group influence   Notion that delinquency is influenced in a greater degree by peer group associations and is commonly applied to male delinquency patterns.

sex-role socialization   Social learning process in which persons are taught behaviors appropriate only for their gender.

Practice Test

Multiple Choice

1. In the vignette at the beginning of this chapter, Noemi was arrested for "armed" robbery using a _____.
   a. gun
   b. knife
   c. screwdriver
   d. baseball bat
   e. night stick

2. The _____ proposes that the gender gap in crime decreases and females account for a greater proportion of crime when women's economic well-being declines.
   a. feminists theory
   b. economic marginalization thesis
   c. the buck stops here thesis
   d. economic disparity thesis

3. What percentage of females in the juvenile justice system are minorities?
   a. 20%
   b. 33%
   c. 40%
   d. 50%
   e. 66%

4. Cesare Lombroso wrote a book about female crime called _____.
   a. *The Fall of Eve*
   b. *The Female Criminal*
   c. *The Female Offender*
   d. *The Mind of a Women Offender*
   e. *The Criminal Female Mind*

5. What year did Cesare Lombroso write his book about women in crime?
a. 1903
b. 1923
c. 1943
d. 1963
e. 1983

6. Cesare Lombroso suggested that women _____.
a. are sexually cold
b. weak
c. have an undeveloped intelligence
d. all of the above

7. Who wrote *Sex and Society*?
a. W.I. Thomas
b. Sigmund Freud
c. Otto Pollak
d. Gisela Konopka
e. Karl Marx

8. According to W.I. Thomas, maleness is _____.
a. social
b. genetic
c. anabolic
d. katabolic
e. none of the above

9. According to W.I. Thomas, femaleness is _____.
a. social
b. genetic
c. anabolic
d. katabolic
e. none of the above

10. Anabolic means all but one of the following.
a. motionless
b. lethargic
c. aggressive
d. conservative

11. Who is the author of *The Unadjusted Girl*?
a. W.I. Thomas
b. Sigmund Freud
c. Otto Pollak
d. Gisela Konopka
e. Karl Marx

12. One of the following is not one of the four wishes or ambitions girls are driven for according to W. I. Thomas.
a. desires for new experiences
b. desire for power
c. desire for security
d. desire for response
e. desire for recognition

13. According to W.I. Thomas, the major cause of prostitution rest in the girls need for _____.
a. sex
b. money
c. attention
d. love
e. power

14. The delinquent girl is one that is attempting to be a man. Which of the following authors would agree with that statement?
a. Albert Cohen
b. Sigmund Freud
c. Otto Pollak
d. Gisela Konopka
e. Karl Marx

15. The author of *The Criminality of Women* is _____.
a. W.I. Thomas
b. Sigmund Freud
c. Otto Pollak
d. Gisela Konopka
e. Karl Marx

16. This book advanced the theory that women are more criminal than is usually believed, but that their crimes largely go unreported or are hidden.
a. *The Unadjusted Girl*
b. *Sex and Society*
c. *The Female Criminal*
d. *The Fall of Eve*
e. *The Criminality of Women*

17. When the police and the court forgive or ignore a crime for which they would convict a boy it is known as _____.
a. abuse of power
b. the gallantry factor
c. the father factor
d. the daughter factor
e. the chivalry factor

18. Emmy Werner and Ruth Smith found in their longitudinal study that _____ was a good predictor of delinquency in girls.
a. grade point average
b. teen pregnancy
c. emotional instability
d. birth order
e. income

19. Freda Adler argued in 1975 that a rise in crime among adult women and juvenile females was clearly linked to _____.
a. discrimination in the workplace
b. opportunity
c. genetics
d. I.Q.
e. gang membership

20. The social learning process in which persons are taught behaviors appropriate only for their sex is called _____.
a. sex-role socialization
b. stereotyping
c. sex norm socialization
d. training of sex

True/False:

1. "High self-esteem encourages definitions favorable to the risk-taking among females but discourages these definitions among males."

2. The second step along females' pathways into the juvenile justice system is victimization.

3. Some feminist theorists propose treating gender as both a key element of social organization and as an individual trait.

4. In many cases, the first step along females' pathways into the juvenile justice system is victimization.

5. Cesare Lombroso contended that because most women are born with "feminine" characteristics, their innate physiological limitations protect them from crime and predispose them to live unimaginative, dull, and conforming lives.

6. The delinquent girl, in the Freudian perspective, is one that is attempting to be a man.

7. Susan Datesman and colleagues found that the perception of limited opportunity was more strongly related to male delinquency than it was to female delinquency.

8. Strain theory has been applied to female delinquents to explain much of their criminal behavior.

9. Freda Adler argued in 1975 that a rise in crime among adult women and juvenile females was clearly linked to a lack of opportunity for females in the workplace.

10. The Marxist theorists would argue that the reason for girls turning to prostitution is the social and economic inequities of a patriarchal capitalist system.

Fill-in-the-blank:

1. The idea that the justice system treated adolescent females and women more leniently because of their gender is called the _____.

2. An argument made by Meda Chesney-Lind and others that adolescent females' victimization at home causes them to become delinquent is called the _____.

3. The personal traits, social positions, and values and beliefs that members of a society attach to being male or female are called _____.

4. Societal definitions of what constitutes masculine and feminine behavior is known as _____.

5. The idea that as girls become more boy-like and acquire more "masculine" traits they become more delinquent is called the _____.

6. The impact of the values and behaviors of fellow age-group members on teenagers' involvement in delinquency is called _____.

7. The process by which boys and girls internalize their culture's norms, sanctions, and expectations for members of their gender is called _____.

Essay:

1. Explain the key features that distinguish feminist theories from other perspectives.

2. What are the four wishes or ambitions that W.I. Thomas suggested girls were driven by.

3. Konopka identified four key factors contributing to female delinquency. What are those four factors?

Answers Practice Test

Multiple Choice:
1. Answer: c   2. Answer: b   3. Answer: e   4. Answer: c   5. Answer: a   6. Answer: d
7. Answer: a   8. Answer: d   9. Answer: c   10. Answer: c   11. Answer: a   12. Answer: b
13. Answer: d   14. Answer: b   15. Answer: c   16. Answer: e   17. Answer: e
18. Answer: c   19. Answer: b   20. Answer: a

True/False:
1. False 2. False   3. False   4. True   5. True   6. True   7. False   8. False   9. False
10. True

Fill-in-the-blank:
1. chivalry factor
2. feminist theory of delinquency
3. gender
4. gender roles
5. masculinity hypothesis
6. peer group influence
7. sex-role socialization

WEBSITES

Read the OJJDP publication, *Juvenile Female Offenders: A Status of the States Report,* at www.justicestudies.com/weblibrary

Read the OJJDP publication, *Guiding Principles for Promising Female Programming: An Inventory of Best Practices,* at www.justicestudies.com/weblibrary

Visit the Center on Juvenile and Criminal Justice, and learn about girls in the criminal justice system via www.justicestudies.com/webplaces

www.academicinfo.net/uswomenrights.html

www.criminolgy.fsu.edu/crimtheory/tedeschi/criminological.htm

CHAPTER 8: THE FAMILY AND DELINQUENCY

LEARNING OBJECTIVES

After reading this chapter, you should be able to answer the following questions:

1. How do problems in the family affect adolescents?

2. What factors in the family are most likely to affect the likelihood of delinquent behavior?

3. What are the main forms of child abuse and neglect?

4. What is the relationship of child abuse and neglect to delinquency and status offenses?

CHAPTER SUMMARY

American families are filled with multiple problems that include divorce, single-parent families, blended families, out-of-wedlock births, alcohol and drug abuse, poverty and violence. The more family related problems an adolescent faces the more likely their chances of becoming delinquent.

Studies on the relationship between family and delinquency generally conclude that quality of life at home is more important than whether or not the home is intact. Parental rejection and inconsistent, lax, or severe discipline are associated with increased delinquency. Accumulation of unfavorable factors within the family increases the propensity of delinquent behavior among children.

The concept of parental supremacy rights has perpetuated the mistreatment of children by their parents. The state has been reluctant to interfere in families unless severe injuries or situations have occurred. Additionally, the acceptability of violence in society and social isolation, especially of lower-class families, has further contributed to the mistreatment of children.

Mandatory reporting measures and funding of treatment programs are aimed at reducing family violence, and creating public awareness to the nature and extent of the abuse problem. Research findings have consistently linked child abuse and neglect to delinquent behavior and status offenses. Abused children runaway from home and become involved in truancy, disruptive school behaviors, drug and alcohol abuse, deviant sexual behaviors, and aggressive acts toward others.

A number of strategies are called for to reduce the extent of child abuse and neglect in the United States. Among those strategies, Cathy Spitz Widom recommends six principles that are needed to tailor the effective treatment of child abuse; (1) earlier interventions, (2) not neglecting children, (3) what works with one child may not work with another, (4) sensitivity to differential treatment on the basis of race or ethnic backgrounds, (5) interventions must be continual, and (6) resources should be accessible.

LECTURE OUTLINE

Introduction:
- Eleven year old sells heroin.

I. The Family and Delinquency
- The importance of family as a contributing factor has varied: (1900-1932) role of the family was emphasized, (1933-1950) the role of family was minimized and the focus shifted to school, social class, and influence of peers, and (1950-1972) there was revised interest in the family.

A. The Broken Home
- Debate rages; however studies indicate delinquency is 10 to 15 percent higher in broken homes. The type of family breakup affects delinquency (divorce is the highest, death is the lowest). Broken homes are not related to gender or age differences, and there is no consistent relationship to the negative impact of Stepparents as often cited.

B. Birth Order
- Some evidence supports that middle children are more likely to be delinquent, in that parents guard the first child more closely and are more experienced with the last child.

C. Family Size
- The larger the family, the more likely the delinquency. Parents are unable to effectively supervise larger families (often delegating older children to help) and they typically have fewer finances.

D. Delinquent Siblings or Criminal Parents
- Siblings seem to learn delinquency from other siblings and significant others. Children of fathers with criminal records are more likely to be poor and have an increased risk for an early first conviction.

E. Quality of Home Life
- Good marital relationships are consistent with strong family cohesiveness.
- Happiness of marriage is key to whether children engage in delinquency.

F. Family Rejection
- Parental rejection is related to delinquency. Rejection by the father appears to be more significant than mother's rejection.

G. Discipline in the Home

- Inadequate supervision is related to delinquency. Discipline that is too strict, too lax, and inconsistent were all associated with increased delinquency.

H. Family Factors and Delinquency
- Overall broken homes, birth order, family size, delinquent siblings, quality of life, family rejection, and home discipline appear to be instrumental in rates of delinquency for juvenile offenders.

II. Child Abuse and Neglect
- Child abuse and neglect is in the form of: (1) physical, (2) sexual, (3) verbal, and (4) psychological. One form of maltreatment often leads to another form.
- Being abused increased the likelihood of juvenile arrest by 59 percent, adult arrest by 29 percent, and arrest for violent crime by 30 percent.
- Maltreated children were younger at time of their arrest and committed twice as many offenses.
- Physically abused and neglected children were most likely to arrested for violent crime.
- Abused and neglected females were also an increased risk.
- The rate for African-American children is more affected by abuse than for white children.

A. Extent and Nature of Child Abuse and Neglect
- Passing of legislation in the 1960s focused national attention on the issue.
- Child Abuse and Prevention Act and the National Center on Child Abuse 1974 focused further attention on abuse problems.
- Neglect is the most common form of Maltreatment.
- Mothers are more likely to neglect children than fathers alone.
- Neglectful mothers include; apathetic-futile, impulse-ridden, mentally retarded, reaction depression, and psychotic.
- Neglectful mother is likely to have been neglected as a child.

1. Physical and Emotional Abuse
- Most common forms include; slapping, spanking, hitting with objects, grabbing, and shoving. Mothers hit children more than fathers do.
- Parents who were hit as children are more likely to hit as parents.
- Corporal punishment legitimizes violence (Straus).
- Emotional abuse involves a disregard for the psychological needs. May include a steady diet of put downs, humiliation, labeling, name-calling, scapegoating, lying, demanding excessive responsibility, seductive behavior, ignoring, fear-inducing techniques, unrealistic expectations, and extreme inconsistency.

2. Nature of Abuse
- Five explanations; (1) structural factors, (2) mental illness of parents, (3) history of abuse as a child, (4) transitory situational factors and (5) a particularly demanding or problematic child.
- Incidence of abuse increases with the child's age, however the more serious cases occur with infants and young children.

- More prevalent in urban areas than rural areas, which may be linked to better reporting methods.
- Often one parent is aggressive, while the other is passive.

3. Sexual Abuse
- Any sexual activity that involves physical contact or sexual arousal between nonmarried members of a family. Includes; oral-genital contact, fondling, masturbation, and intercourse.
- Gordon's examination revealed 98 percent of the cases were father-daughter incest in which girl victims became second wives.
- The average incestuous relationship last three to four years.
- Mother-son incest is less common and rarely reported. Father-son is also rare.
- Justice and Justice study suggests that; fathers with symbiotic personalities make up 70 to 80 percent of incestuous fathers. They have a strong need for warmth and a sense of belonging, use rationalizations to justify their actions. With the psychopathic father sex is simply a vehicle to express hostility. Pedophilic personalities have erotic cravings and do not want rejection. Psychotic fathers come from a subculture that permits incest.

B. Abuse, Neglect and Delinquency
- Abused and neglected children are more likely to become involved in status offenses of truancy, disruptive school behaviors, running away and drugs/alcohol offenses.

1. Emotional Trauma of Child Abuse and Neglect
- Characterized as having low self-esteem, considerable guilt, high anxiety, mild to serious depression, and high internal conflict.
- Experience sleep disturbances, weight loss or gain, poor social relationships.

2. Runaways
- Abused teens frequently escape their situation by running away. The pattern of escaping often continues even when placed into foster care.

3. Disruptive and Truant Behavior in School
- Abused children have more difficulty in school and tend to become academic and social failures. Suffer deficiencies in language, concentrating and often destructive of property.

4. Drug and Alcohol Abuse
- Many abused children turn to drug and alcohol abuse to blot out pain. Often feel they have nothing to lose and only want to forget their insecurities.

5. Sexual Behavior
- One study revealed 66 percent of pregnant teens had been sexually abused. Victims tend to be sexually promiscuous and favor prostitution, especially male prostitutes.

6. **Violence and Abuse**
   - Male victims tend express outward acts of violence, while female victims tend to engage in self-destructive behaviors.
   - Those that were abused as children also tend to abuse as adults.

III. The Family and the Life Course
   - Parental support and control are intertwined for parental efficacy (Wright/Cullen).
   - Ineffective parents fail to monitor children and fail to punish deviance.
   - Coercive discipline may teach children that force and violence are appropriate tactics.

IV. Child Abuse and the Juvenile Justice System
   - Child protective services differ in procedures. Typically includes: identification, reporting, intake and investigation, assessment, case planning, treatment, evaluation of family progress, case closure, and prosecution.
   - Reporting often required by law. Service staff required to determine how urgent the response is needed. Police are frequently involved to protect workers and gather evidence. If imminent risk is determined, a temporary removal hearing will occur. Case planning will design a treatment plan and will close a case for successful treatment of the family or refusal of the family to cooperate (in mild cases).
   - Adjudication is held in which the charge of abuse or neglect is either substantiated or disposed of. Supremacy of parental rights has widespread support among juvenile judges. Prosecution depends on the severity of the abuse.
   - Abuse and neglect cases are more likely to be reported among lower-class families.
   - Delinquency in America: A Parent's Right to Know

KEY TERMS

birth order   A notion that middle children are more prone to delinquency than the first or last-born.

broken home   Early view, which holds that homes broken by divorce, separation, and death are more likely to produce delinquency than intact homes.

brother-sister incest   Suggested to be the most frequently occurring type of incest, and believed to be less damaging than father-daughter incest.

child abuse   Encompasses many dimensions with the general focus being variations of physical, sexual, emotional, and verbal abuse typically perpetrated by adults against children.

delinquent siblings   The notion that having delinquent sisters and brothers will increase the propensity of delinquency within the home by influencing the other sibling(s).

emotional abuse   Any action that reduces the self-esteem and psychological well-being of a child normally inflicted by parents and adults, and directed toward children.

family size   The number of children in a family; a possible risk factor for delinquency.

father-daughter incest   The most devastating form of incest in which the father frequently views the daughter as a second wife.

father-son incest   Sexual activity between father and son.

mother-son incest   Sexual activity that occurs between mother and son.

neglect   A disregard for the physical, emotional, or moral needs of children. Child neglect involves the failure of the parent of caregiver to provide nutritious food, adequate clothing and sleeping arrangements, essential medical care, sufficient supervision, access to education, and normal experiences that produce feelings of being loved, wanted secure, and worthy.

rejection by parents   Disapproval, repudiation, or other uncaring behavior directed by parents toward children; it can be a factor in delinquency.

sexual abuse   Intentional and wrongful physical contact with a person, with or without his or her consent, that entails a sexual purpose or component. In the study of adolescence, the term generally refers to any sexual activity that involves physical contact or sexual contact between members of a family who are not married to one another, and especially to such contact between a parent and his or her children; also know as incest.

socialization   The process by which individuals come to internalize their culture; through this process an individual learns the norms, sanctions, and expectations of being a member of a particular society.

supervision and discipline   The parental monitoring, guidance, and control of children's activities and behavior. Unfair and inconsistent supervision and discipline often are associated with delinquency.

Practice Test

Multiple Choice:

1. In the vignette, at the beginning of the chapter, the authorities were considering charging an eleven year old girl with the crime of _____.
a. murder
b. rape
c. selling heroin
d. shop lifting
e. prostitution

2. The primary agent for the socialization of children is _____.
a. the church
b. the school
c. the gang
d. the family
e. the peer group

3. The structural perspective focuses on factors such as _____.
a. parental absence
b. family size
c. birth order
d. all of the above

4. The functional perspective focuses on factors such as _____.
a. the degree of marital happiness
b. the amount and type of discipline
c. the significance of parent- child interaction
d. all of the above

5. In 1924, George B. Mangold declared, "The _____ is probably the single most important cause of delinquency".
a. broken home
b. the school
c. the church
d. the gang
e. the pool hall

6. As far as delinquency and birth order is concerned, it is more likely that the _____ will become delinquent.
a. first child
b. middle children
c. last child
d. birth order is not related to delinquency

7. Research findings on family size generally reveal that _____ families have more delinquency.
a. small
b. middle size
c. large
d. family size has no relationship to delinquency

8. According to your text, the affect of the movie *Colors* was _____.
a. gang members quit wearing colors because they could be identified by the police.
b. gang members increased the use of wearing colors
c. to cause gang members to change their colors
d. to cause police officers to begin to wear colors.

9. Craig A. Anderson has concluded that aggressive video games _____.
a. make juveniles better students
b. have no affect on a juveniles tendency to be delinquent
c. makes juveniles less delinquent
d. leads to aggressive behavior

10. A form of Hip Hop music that some believe negatively influences young people by devaluing human life, the family, religious institutions, schools, and the justice system is called _____.
a. Gangsta Rap
b. Rock and Roll
c. Hard Rock
d. Alterative Rock
e. all of the above

11. When a caretaker fails to ensure that a child receives adequate education it is called _____.
a. physical abuse
b. physical neglect
c. emotional maltreatment
d. educational maltreatment
e. moral-legal maltreatment

12. When a caretaker exposes a child to or involves a child in illegal or other activities that may foster delinquency or antisocial behavior it is called _____.
a. physical abuse
b. physical neglect
c. emotional maltreatment
d. educational maltreatment
e. moral-legal maltreatment

13. When a caretaker fails to exercise a minimum degree of care in meeting a child's physical needs it is called _____.
a. physical abuse
b. physical neglect
c. emotional maltreatment
d. educational maltreatment
e. moral-legal maltreatment

14. According to your text, who first exposed child abuse as a major social problem?
a. Norman A. Polansky
b. C. H. Kempe
c. Michael Gottfredson and Travis Hirschi's
d. Craig A. Anderson
e. George B. Mangold

!5. Which of the following groups have the highest rate of maltreatment of children?
a. African Americans
b. whites
c. Hispanic
d. Asian
e. American Indian

16. In 2004, approximately how many children died in America of neglect or abuse?
a.   238
b.   387
c.   519
d.   960
e. 1490

17. The disregard for the physical, emotional, or moral needs of children or adolescents is called

_____.
a. physical abuse
b. physical neglect
c. neglect
d. educational maltreatment
e. moral-legal maltreatment

18. Norman A. Polansky and colleagues' studies of neglect in Georgia and North Carolina identified five types of mothers who are frequently guilty of child neglect. A mother that is borderline or psychotic is _____.
a. emotionally numb to her children and neglects both their physical and emotional needs
b. restless and craves excitement, movement and change. She is unable to tolerate stress or frustration and is aggressive and defiant.
c. a mentally retarded mother who has difficulty providing adequate care for her children
d. lost in her fantasies and may forget to feed the children or may even kill the children and herself in a psychotic outburst

19. Norman A. Polansky and colleagues' studies of neglect in Georgia and North Carolina identified five types of mothers who are frequently guilty of child neglect. A mother who is impulse-ridden is _____.
a. emotionally numb to her children and neglects both their physical and emotional needs
b. restless and craves excitement, movement and change. She is unable to tolerate stress or frustration and is aggressive and defiant.
c. a mentally retarded mother who has difficulty providing adequate care for her children
d. lost in her fantasies and may forget to feed the children or may even kill the children and herself in a psychotic outburst

20. Norman A. Polansky and colleagues' studies of neglect in Georgia and North Carolina identified five types of mothers who are frequently guilty of child neglect. A mother who is a apathetic-futile mother is _____.
a. emotionally numb to her children and neglects both their physical and emotional needs
b. restless and craves excitement, movement and change. She is unable to tolerate stress or frustration and is aggressive and defiant.
c. a mentally retarded mother who has difficulty providing adequate care for her children
d. lost in her fantasies and may forget to feed the children or may even kill the children and herself in a psychotic outburst

21. Murray Straus defines corporal punishment as _____.
a. good parenting
b. regretful, but necessary to control the deviant child
c. proper parent if use only sparingly
d. physical abuse
e. all of the above

22. Child abuse seems more prevalent in _____.
a. urban areas
b. suburban areas
c. rural areas
d. child abuse is equally distributed between these areas

23. Intentional and wrongful physical contact with a person, with or without his or her consent, that entails a sexual purpose or component is called _____.
a. sexual abuse
b. sexual play
c. sexual masturbation
d. sexual intercourse
e. sexual arousal

24. The National Center on Child Abuse and Neglect defines _____ as "intrafamily sexual abuse which is perpetrated on a child by a member of that child's family group."
a. sexual abuse
b. sexual play
c. incest
d. sexual intercourse
e. sexual arousal

25. During the Clinton administration (1992-2000) sexual abuse cases _____.
a. decreased by 40%
b. increased by 40%
c. remained at an all time high
d. increased, but only by a few percentage points
e. decrease, but only by a few percentage points

26. According to Justice and Justice, incestuous fathers who have strong unmet needs for warmth and for someone to whom they can be close are called _____.
a. symbolic personalities
b. psychopathic personalities
c. pedophilic personalities
d. psychotic fathers

27. Victims of child abuse and neglect often have
a. low self-esteem
b. considerable guilt
c. high anxiety and mild to serious depression
d. high internal conflict
e. all of the above

28. Michael Gottfredson and Travis Hirschi's self-control theory argues that the principal cause of individuals' low self-control is _____.
a. the lack of religion in schools
b. the lack of discipline in schools
c. ineffective parenting
d. punishments that are too liberal
e. all of the above

True/False:

1. The structural perspective focuses on factors such as parent child interaction, the degree of marital happiness, and the amount and type of discipline.

2. In 1924, George B. Mangold declared, The broken home is probably the single most important cause of delinquency.

3. There is no evidence that supports the idea that birth order is related to delinquent behavior.

4. Research findings on family size generally reveal that small families have more delinquency than large families.

5. W. L. Slocum and C. L. Stone discover that children from affectionate homes tend to be more conforming in behavior.

6. The father-child bond is not more predictive of juvenile's involvement in crime, especially among the boys.

7. Hirschi found that the rate of delinquency increased with the incidence of mothers' employed outside the home.

8. Between 1980 and 1994 the rate of child barring by unmarried women rose sharply for women of all ages.

9. B. F. Steele's study of 200 juvenile first-time offenders found that between 70 and 80 percent had a history of neglect and abuse.

10. A mother who is impulse-ridden is emotionally numb to her children and neglects both their physical and emotional needs.

11. One of the reasons that Murray Straus supports corporal punishment is that failure to use it damages the child far more than using corporal punishment.

12. Child abuse seems to be more prevalent in urban areas than in suburban or rural settings.

13. Teenagers who have been abused frequently run away from home.

14. Several studies have found that abused and neglected children have more success in school than children who are not abused.

15. One of the consistent conclusions of domestic violence research is that individuals who have experienced violent and abusive childhoods are more likely to grow up and become child and spouse abusers than individuals who have experienced little or no violence in their childhood.

Fill-in-the-blank

1. A notion that middle children are more prone to delinquency than the first or last-born is because of their _____.

2. An early view, which holds that homes broken by divorce, separation, and death are more likely to produce delinquency than intact homes is called _____.

3. Suggested to be the most frequently occurring type of incest, and believed to be less damaging than father-daughter incest is _____.

4. _____ encompasses many dimensions with the general focus being variations of physical, sexual, emotional, and verbal abuse typically perpetrated by adults against children.

5. The notion that having delinquent sisters and brothers will increase the propensity of delinquency within the home by influencing the other sibling(s) is the idea of _____.

6. Any action that reduces the self-esteem and psychological well-being of a child normally inflicted by parents and adults, and directed toward children is _____.

7. The number of children in a family sometimes called _____, is a possible risk factor for delinquency.

8. The most devastating form of incest in which the father frequently views the daughter as a second wife is called _____.

9. Sexual activity between father and son is called _____.

10. Sexual activity that occurs between mother and son is called _____.

11. A disregard for the physical, emotional, or moral needs of children is _____.

12. Disapproval, repudiation, or other uncaring behavior directed by parents toward children which can factor in delinquency is _____.

13. Intentional and wrongful physical contact with a person, with or without his or her consent, that entails a sexual purpose or component is called _____.

14. The process by which individuals come to internalize their culture; through _____, an individual learns the norms, sanctions, and expectations of being a member of a particular society.

15. Often associated with delinquency, the parental monitoring, guidance, and control of children's activities and behavior involving unfair and inconsistent supervision is known as _____.

Answer: supervision and discipline

Essay:

1. The Child Maltreatment 2004 survey identified several factor that influenced the determination that a child would officially be found to a victim of maltreatment. What are those factors?

2. Norman A. Polansky and colleagues' studies of neglect in Georgia and North Carolina identified five types of mothers who are frequently guilty of child neglect. Explain each of those five types of mothers.

3. Some theorists argue that child abuse has five basic explanations: What are those five basic explanations?

4. David g. gill, in developing a classification of abusive families, found that seven situations accounted for 97.3 percent of the reported abuse cases. What are those seven classifications?

5. Justice and Justice have developed a classification that is helpful in understanding the behavior of fathers who commit incest. They divide incestuous fathers into four groups. Explain each of those four groups.

Answers Practice Test

Multiple Choice:
1. Answer: c   2. Answer: d   3. Answer: d   4. Answer: d   5. Answer: a   6. Answer: b
7. Answer: c   8. Answer: b   9. Answer: d   10. Answer: a   11. Answer: d   12. Answer: e
13. Answer: b   14. Answer: b   15. Answer: a   16. Answer: e   17. Answer: c
18. Answer: d   19. Answer: b   20. Answer: a   21. Answer: d   22. Answer: a
23. Answer: a   24. Answer: c   25. Answer: a   26: Answer: a   27. Answer: a
28. Answer: c

True/False:
1. False 2. True 3. False 4. False 5. True 6. True 7. True 8. True 9. True
10. False 11. False 12. True 13. True 14. False 15. True

Fill-in-the-blank:
1. birth order
2. broken homes
3. brother-sister incest
4. child abuse
5. delinquent siblings
6. emotional abuse
7. family size
8. father-daughter incest
9. father-son incest
10. mother-son incest
11. neglect
12. rejection by parents
13. sexual abuse
14. socialization
15. supervision and discipline

WEBSITES:

Read the NIJ-sponsored publication, *Communitywide Strategies to Reduce child abuse and Neglect: Lessons from the Safe Kids/Safe Streets Program,* at www.justicestudies.com/weblibrary

Read the NIJ-sponsored publication, *Co-Occurring Intimate Partner Violence and Child Maltreatment ,* at www.justicestudies.com/weblibrary

Visit the Center on Child Abuse and Neglect's Web site via www.justicestudies.com/webplaces

Visit the Child Welfare League of America's Web site via www.justicestudies.com/webplaces

Visit the National Center for Missing and Exploited Children's Web site via www.justicestudies.com/webplaces

Visit the National Clearinghouse on Child Neglect Information via www.justicestudies.com/webplaces

Visit the Child Exploitation and Obscenity Section of the U.S. Department of Justice's Criminal Division via www.justicestudies.com/webplaces

Visit the Family Violence and Sexual Assault Institute's Web site via www.justicestudies.com/webplaces

Visit the National Center for Children Exposed to Violence via www.justicestudies.com/webplaces

www.childabuse.org

www.angelfire.com/ar/jotsntitles

CHAPTER 9: THE SCHOOL AND DELINQUENCY

LEARNING OBJECTIVES

After reading this chapter, you should be able to answer the following questions:

1. How has education evolved over time in the United States?

2. What is the relationship between delinquency and school failure?

3. What theoretical perspectives related to the school experience best explain delinquency?

4. What rights do school students have?

5. How has the partnership between the school and the justice system changed?

6. Which intervention strategies seem to be the most promising in the school setting?

CHAPTER SUMMARY

The chapter examines the relationship between school and delinquency. School has long been acknowledged as an important socializing agent in the lives of children, but public education is under sharp criticism for contributing to the delinquency of children. Public schools are accused of failing in their task of educating and properly socializing youth in the United States. The baby boom of the 1950s brought large numbers of school-aged children into the educational systems during the 1960s and 1970s.

The pervasiveness of *vandalism* and *violence* in public education came to public attention by the mid 1970s. Assaults on students increased, and crime costs associated with vandalism and violence soared. The 1980s brought to public attention a new form of school violence in which teachers and school officials were now part of the victimization group. Open locker searches revealed students bringing a variety of destructive paraphernalia to schools including, drugs, knives, guns, and dynamite. By the 1990s students are regularly reporting high fear levels. Metal detectors are commonplace and the incidences of school violence are perpetuated by national stories on school shootings, which are claiming the lives of unsuspecting students and teachers. Gang intimidation and other fear factors are now motivating students to report to school with armaments for their own sense of protection.

Various theoretical perspectives offer explanations to help understand the impact of school on delinquent behavior. For schools in the United States to improve, a number of changes involving complex socialization processes must take place. These changes include evaluating the quality of the school experience, providing more *alternative schools* for *disruptive students*, finding ways to renew urban schools, developing more positive social-community relationships, and making schools safe havens from violence.

LECTURE OUTLINE

Introduction
- The story of Jess Weise: Murder on an Indian Reservation

I. A History of American Education
- By 1918 nearly every state has compulsory education laws.
- John Dewey advocated reform in classroom methods/curriculum in early 1900s.
- The impact of the 1954 U.S. Court decision on school segregation issues.
- The baby boom of the 1950s increased school enrollments in 1960s and 1970s.

II. School Crime

A. Vandalism and Violence
- Schools lodged in unsafe neighborhoods are in the center of gang communities and drug infested areas.
- Repressive methods of education fail to work with learning disabled children. Conventional education leads to boredom, frustration and alienation with LD students.
- Authoritarian schools have taught some lower functioning students to loose themselves in the crowd (like inmates).
- Added security in schools make them appear more like prisons.
- Ruled unconstitutional in Boston for every student to be drug tested.
- Vandalism and violence in schools comes to public attention in 1970s. Senate subcommittee investigates with report published in 1978. 36 percent of all assaults on 12 to 19 year olds occurred in school. Total crime cost $200 million per year.
- 1980s adds a new dimension of violence directed against teachers and school officials. Acts include threats of murder, rape, physical assault, arson and destruction of personal property. 1988 NASHS survey reported that; over one-third of students had been threatened at school, one-seventh of students were robbed, one-half of males and one-quarter of females had been in at least one fist-fight at school, a weapon was involved in one-third of the crimes.
- NCVS in 1989 reveals similar type of victimization statistics.
- 1993 CDC survey reveals students missed a day a school for their own safety, and 22 percent carried some type of weapon for safety.
- 2002 annual report on school safety by the Department of Justice and Education provided the following profile: chance of suffering a school-associated death is low, students aged 12 to 18 suffer violent victimization at a rate of 5 per 1000 students.
- Social policy: Indicators of School Crime and Safety 2005

III. Delinquency and School Failure
- Lack of achievement, low social status, and high dropout rate are the factors most frequently cited as related to delinquents failing at school.

A. Achievement in School
- Poor academic performance is related to both male and female delinquency.
- Good relationships with teachers, students, and administrators may reduce vandalism and increase achievement in school.

B. Social Status
- A. Cohen's study with working-class boys reveals that lower-class youth may rebel against middle-class values when frustrated over inability to achieve.
- Some studies suggest association between status and school failure may not be as strong as once thought.
- Delinquency in America: Black Youths Learn to Make the Right Moves

C. The School Dropout
- Poor grades are predictors for dropping out of school.
- Males are more likely than females. Minorities are more likely than whites.
- Dropouts have higher rates of police contact.
- Relationship is multidimensional. Dropouts make less money and have fewer job prospects, are prone to delinquency, more welfare dependent, experience more unstable marriages.
- Delinquency may be caused by school dropout or nonschool reasons such as, personal, environmental, and economic conditions.

IV. Theoretical Perspectives on School and Delinquency
- *Cultural deviance theories* argue children learn deviance through social exposure to others and modeling.
- *Strain theory* contends lower-class students are denied legitimate means to achieve society's goals. Students in turn compensate for feelings of failure and low self-esteem.
- *Social control theorists* suggest delinquency varies according to the strength of the juvenile's bonds to the social order, thus delinquency will result if the bonds do not develop.
- *Labeling theorists* state that as negative labels are assigned to students, that students react accordingly with aggression for differential treatment by school authorities.
- *Marxists* view school as a means in which the privileged classes maintain control over the lower classes. Lower-class children are taught to accept menial roles.

V. Student Rights
- Concept of *loco parentis* in which school authority stands in the place of parents.
- Courts have become involved in areas of: procedural due process, freedom of expression, hair/dress codes, and safety.

A. Procedural Due Process
- *Dixon v. Alabama State Board of Education* results in requirement for due process notification before a student is expelled for misconduct.
- *Goss v. Lopez* case holds that fair fact-finding must precede suspension notices. The *Wood v. Strickland* case found school officials are subject to civil suit for deliberately depriving students of constitutional rights.

B. Freedom of Expression
- *Tinker V. Des Moines* Independent School District holds students have the right to express themselves (black armbands in Vietnam era).
- *W. Virginia State Board of Education v. Barnette* states students could not be compelled to salute the flag.

C. Hair and Dress Codes
- *Yoo v. Moynihan* holds that students have the right to style their hair.
- *Richards v. Thurston* states the right to wear long hair. Other similar cases have prohibited schools from disallowing of slacks, dungarees, etc.

D. School Searches
- *New Jersey v. TLO* in 1985 allowed searches of students lockers and paved the way for random drug testing in schools (*Vernonia School District 47 v. Acton*).
- In 2002, the Court extended the drug testing of students in extracurricular activities.

E. Safety
- School officials have become reluctant to suspend youths for acting insubordinate and creating classroom disturbances that only a few decades earlier would have drawn quick suspension or expulsion.
- In sum, judicial intervention has had both positive and negative impacts.

VI. School and Justice System Partnerships
- Police sponsored programs such as DARE and PAL, along with gang education and training are aimed at crime prevention today rather than education.
- Per U.S. Department of Education's report in 1997: 97 percent of schools use some form of security measures. Shift in language: officers are brought in to *fight campus crime, zero tolerance, combat victimization* etc.
- Focus on investigation, drug sweeps, surveillances and crowd control. (STAR program)

VII. Promising Intervention Strategies
- Education must be oriented toward the individual and progress not compared to that of others in the class, particularly for low achievers.
- Tracking systems should be abolished.

- Students need to feel safe to become involved in the school experience.
- Good teaching is the first line of defense against misbehavior.

A. Improving the Quality of the School Experience
- The need to orient education toward the individual.
- Tracking systems need abolished as they tend to establish class systems within school.
- The need for quality instruction and flexible schedules.

B. Alternative Schools
- Disadvantaged students require special curriculum materials, smaller classes and individualized tutoring to master presented material.
- Ultimate goal of *alternative schools* is to return students to mainstream education after dealing with disruptive behaviors.
- Effectiveness of schools is mixed. Some of the larger schools such as St. Louis and Chicago are very successful.

C. Positive School-Community Relationships
- Legendary *"blackboard jungle"* an investment in hardware and preventative technology.
- Development of multi-component approaches involving home, school, and other institutions that are involved in students' lives.
- Activities arranged around community involvement with educational systems.

D. School-Based Violence Prevention Programs
- Federal grants needed to implement violence and drug prevention programs.
- Interconnectedness of family, peer group, school, and neighborhood.
- Dynamic interactions between individuals and social contexts.
- Prevention efforts require collaboration.
- Need for public health approach to violence prevention.
- Effective programs and strategies for preventing violence.

E. From Correctional Contexts to School Settings
- New priority of transitioning juvenile offenders back to school and life in the community (Franklin Transitional High School).

KEY TERMS

academic performance   Achievement in schoolwork as rated by grades and other assessment measures. Poor academic performance is a factor in delinquency.

alternative schools   Schools designed to provide alternative educational experiences for youths who are not reaching their academic and behavioral potentials in a traditional school setting.

bullying   Hurtful, frightening or menacing actions undertaken by one person to intimidate another (generally weaker) person, to gain that person's unwilling compliance, and/or to put him in fear.

disruptive behavior   Includes behaviors, which detract from the educational experience such as unwillingness to follow rules, manipulation of teachers, and defiance of authority.

dropout   A public or private school student that chooses no longer to attend school and increases their likelihood of becoming delinquent.

due process rights   Constitutional rights that are guaranteed to citizens-whether adult or juvenile- during their contacts with the people, their proceedings in court, and their interactions with the public school.

in loco parentis   Legal requirement that schools act in place of the parents in providing educational services for children.

school searches   The process of searching students and their lockers to determine whether drugs, weapons or other contraband are present.

vandalism   An act in which person(s) cause damage and destruction to property typically associated with schools or other authority venues, in which the perpetrators may find to be oppressive or repressive.

violence   An act aimed at serious injury of another, and often perpetrated against students and school officials thereby reducing the quality of the educational experience.

Practice Test

Multiple Choice:

1. In the vignette at the beginning of the chapter, 16 year old Jess Weise killed his _____.
a. teacher
b. mother
c. grandfather
d. girlfriend
e. neighbor

2. Eric Harris and Dylan Klebold are best know for _____.
a. the shooting at Columbine High School
b. the shootings at Red Lake Indian Reservation
c. the shootings at Santana High School
d. the shootings at Westside Middle School, Jonesboro, Arkansas
e. Wheeling High School. Wheeling, WV

3. At the turn of the twentieth century there was widespread dissatisfaction with the schools which create the _____ education movement.
a. modern
b. traditional
c. conservative
d. liberal
e. progressive

4. John Dewey founded the _____ education movement.
a. modern
b. traditional
c. conservative
d. liberal
e. progressive

5. The National Crime Victimization Survey interviewed 10,000 youths in 1989 and concluded that _____ of the students, ages 12-19 were crime victims in or around their school the previous six-month period.
a. 1%
b. 3.%
c. 5%
d. 7%
e. 9%

6. In a 1995-96 survey, _____ percent of students said they had seen a weapon at school.
a. 10.1
b. 22.1
c. 30.1
d. 38.1
e. 49.1

7. From July 1, 2001, through June 30, 2002, there were _____ homicides of school-age youth (5-19) at school.
a. 17
b. 24
c. 33
d. 41
e. over 50

8 A student chances of being a homicide victim at school is _____.
a. 1 in a   100
b. 1 in a   1,000
c. 1 in   10,000
d. 1 in a   100,000
e. 1 in a 1,000,000

9. Annually, from 1999 through 2003, _____ were more likely to be attacked than other teachers.
a. elementary teachers
b. middle school teachers
c. senior high school
d. community college teachers
e. college professors

10. Maguin and Loeber found that children with lover academic performance _____.
a. committed more delinquent acts than those with higher academic performance
b. committed more serious delinquent acts than those with higher academic perfomance
c. had a longer offending history than those with higher academic performance
d. all of the above

11. Who said that working class boys feel status deprivation when they become award that they are unable to compete with middle-class youths in the school?
a. Edwin Sutherland
b. Robert Jones
c. Robert Merton
d. Albert Cohen
e. James Q. Wilson

12. According to a 2001 report on graduation conducted b the Education Policy Center of the Urban Institute, the national graduation rate was _____.
a. 93%
b. 88%
c. 83%
d. 78%
e. 68%

13. Orrin Hudson, a former Alabama state trooper, uses _____ to teach students lessons about life choices.
a. video games
b. chess
c. boxing
d. military boot camp type training
e. all of the above

14. Almost _____ of black men in their 20's are in prison or on probation or parole.
   a. 5%
   b. 10%
   c. 20%
   d. 25%
   e. 33%

15. The Raging Rooks are _____.
   a. a gang in East L.A.
   b. a gang in Brooklyn
   c. a gang in Chicago
   d. a gang in Detroit
   e. none of the above

16. Elliot and Voss discovered that school dropouts _____.
   a. have much higher rates of police contacts
   b. have much higher rates of officially recorded delinquent behavior
   c. have much higher rates of self-reported delinquent behavior
   d. all of the above

17. School dropouts make up _____ of the nation's prison population.
   a. 20%
   b. 30%
   c. 40%
   d. 50%
   e. 60%

18. School dropouts _____.
   a. have fewer job prospects
   b. make lower salaries,
   c. are more often unemployed
   d. more likely to be welfare dependent
   e. all of the above

19. A theory that contents that youngsters from certain social classes are denied legitimate
access to culturally determined goals and opportunities, and that the resulting frustration leads to
the use of illegitimate means to obtain society's goals or rejection of them is called _____.
   a. cultural deviance theory
   b. radical criminology
   c. strain theory
   d. labeling theory
   e. social control theory

20. A theory that argues that children learn delinquent behavior through exposure to others and by mimicking or modeling other's actions is called _____. Children view delinquency as acceptable because of their exposure to others whose definitions of such behavior are positive.
a. cultural deviance theory
b. radical criminology
c. strain theory
d. labeling theory
e. social control theory

21. A theory that argues that delinquency varies according to the strength of a juvenile's bond to the social order is called _____.
a. cultural deviance theory
b. radical criminology
c. strain theory
d. labeling theory
e. social control theory

22. A theory that argues that once students are defined as deviant, they adopt a deviant role in response to their lowered status is called _____.
a. cultural deviance theory
b. radical criminology
c. strain theory
d. labeling theory
e. social control theory

23. A theory that argues that the school is a means by which the privileged classes maintain power over the lower classes is called _____.
a. cultural deviance theory
b. radical criminology
c. strain theory
d. labeling theory
e. social control theory

24. A theory that argues that once self control has formed in childhood , it affects adolescents in the choices they make in peer relations, school conduct and achievement, drug and alcohol use, and delinquent activities is called _____.
a. general theory of crime
b. radical criminology
c. strain theory
d. labeling theory
e. social control theory

25. A legal requirement that schools act in place of the parents in providing educational services for children is called _____.
a. mens rea
b. actus reus
c. in loco parentis
d. parens patriae
e. non prosequitor

26. The case of *Burnside v. Byars* concluded that _____.
a. school officials may not search a student for any reason
b. that school officials must be reasonable in rules and regulations
c. that school officials may use corporal punishment when disciplining children
d. that school officials may not use corporal punishment when disciplining children
e. none of the above

27. What case declared that student do not shed their constitutional rights of freedom of speech at the schoolhouse gate?

a. Burnside v. Byars
b. Dixon v. Alabama State Board of Education
c. Tinker v Des Moines Independent School District
d. New Jersey v. TLO
e. In re Gault

28. What case examined the issue of whether Fourth Amendment rights against unreasonable searches and seizures apply to the school setting?
a. Burnside v. Byars
b. Dixon v. Alabama State Board of Education
c. Tinker v Des Moines Independent School District
d. New Jersey v. TLO
e. In re Gault

29. In the case of _____ the Court ruled that a student's right to style his or her hair was held to be under the definition of the constitutional right to privacy.
a. Burnside v. Byars
b. Dixon v. Alabama State Board of Education
c. Tinker v Des Moines Independent School District
d. New Jersey v. TLO
e. Yoo v. Moynihan

30. In the case of _____ the Court ruled that a school may search by having a random drug-testing policy for student athletes.
a. Burnside v. Byars
b. Vernonia School District 47J v. Acton
c. Tinker v Des Moines Independent School District
d. New Jersey v. TLO
e. Yoo v. Moynihan

True/False:

1. The Center for Disease Control and Prevention (CDC) found that more than 4% of students miss a day of school each month because they feared for their safety.

2. In a 1995-96 survey, only 13 percent of students said that they ever saw a weapon at school.

3. The report, *Indicators of School Crime and Safety: 2005* indicated that schools are safer for children than other areas of their lives.

4. From July 1, 2001, through June 30, 2002, there were 17 homicides of school-age youth (5-19) at school.

5. A student chances of being a homicide victim at school is one in ten thousand.

6. A student is more likely to be a victim of violence at school then anywhere else.

7. Elementary school teachers were more likely than high school teachers to be victims of violent crimes and thefts.

8. In 1999-2000, teachers in central city schools were more likely to have been threatened with injury or physically attacked during the previous 12 months than teachers in urban fringe or rural schools.

9. The 1967 report by the Task Force on Juvenile Delinquency concluded that boys who failed in school were seven times more likely to become delinquent than those who did not fail.

10. There is no evidence that students who violate school standards pertaining to such things as smoking, truancy, tardiness, dress, classroom demeanor, relations with peers, and respect for authority are more likely to become delinquent that those who conform to such standards.

11. Students from disadvantaged minority groups (American Indian, Hispanic, African American have little more than a fifty-fifty chance of finishing high school with a diploma.

12. More males graduate from high school then do females.

13. Almost one-third of black men in their 20's are in prison or on probation or parole.

14. School dropouts will learn $200,000 less that high school graduates, and over $800,000 less than college graduates.

15. School dropouts make up 20% of the nation's prison population.

Fill-in-the-blank:

1. Academic achievement in schoolwork as rated by grades and other assessment measures is known as _____.

2. A facility that provides an alternative educational experience, usually in a different location, for youths who are not doing satisfactory work in the public school setting is know as a/an
_____.

3. Hurtful, frightening, or menacing actions undertaken by one person to intimidate another (generally weaker) person, to gain that person's unwilling compliance, and /or to put him in fear is known as _____.

4. Unacceptable conduct at school; which may include defiance of authority, manipulation of teachers, inability or refusal to follow rules, fights with peers, destruction of property, use of drug, and physical or verbal altercations with teachers is known as _____.

5. A young person of school age who of his or her own volition no longer attends school is known as a _____.

6. Constitutional rights that are guaranteed to citizens, whether adult or juvenile, during their contacts with the police and during court proceedings are known as _____.

7. The principle according to which a guardian or an agency is given the rights, duties, and responsibilities of a parent in relation to a particular child or children is know as _____.

8. The process of searching students and their lockers to determine whether drugs, weapons or other contraband are present is know as a _____.

9. Destroying or attempting to destroy, (except by burning) public property or the property of another, without the owner's consent is known as _____.

10. Forceful physical assault, with or without weapons, which includes fighting, rape, gang warfare, or other attacks is termed _____.

Essay:

1. Write a brief statement explaining why Craig Haney and Philip Zimbardo compare high schools to prisons.

2. Explain in detail the case of New Jersey v. T.L.O..

3. What can schools do to control bullying in the school system?

4. The text gives 40 examples of school related shootings. Please briefly describe 5 of those examples.

5. Describe the report entitled *Indicators of School Crime and Safety: 2005*. How many students do become victims of crime at school?

6. Explain the relationship between school fairer and delinquency.

Answers Practice Test

Multiple Choice:
1. Answer: c   2. Answer: a   3. Answer: e   4. Answer: e   5. Answer: e   6. Answer: e
7. Answer: a   8. Answer: e   9. Answer: c   10. Answer: d   11. Answer: d   12. Answer: e
13. Answer: b   14. Answer: e   15. Answer: e   16. Answer: e   17. Answer: e
18. Answer: e   19. Answer: c   20. Answer: a   21. Answer: e   22. Answer: d
23. Answer: c   24. Answer: a   25. Answer: c   26: Answer: b   27. Answer: c
28. Answer: d   29. Anwer: e   30: Answer: b

True/False:
1. True 2. False 3. True 4. True 5. False 6. False 7. False 8. True 9. True
10. False   11. True   12. False   13. True   14. True   15. False

Fill-in-the-blank:
1. academic performance
2. alternative school
3. bullying
4. disruptive behavior
5. dropout
6. due process rights
7. in loco parentis
8. school search
9. vandalism
10. violence

137

WEBSITES

Read the OJJDP Fact Sheet, *Overcoming Barriers to school Reentry,* at
www.justicestudies.com/weblibrary

Read the Bureau of Justice Statistics (BJS) publication, *Indicators of School Crime and Safety,* at
www.justicestudies.com/weblibrary

Read the NIJ-sponsored publication, *Effectiveness of School-Based Violence Prevention Programs for Reducing Disruptive and aggressive Behavior,* at
www.justicestudies.com/weblibrary

Read the Office of Community Oriented Policing Services (COPS) publication, *Bullying in Schools,* at www.justicestudies.com/weblibrary

Read the OJJDP Fact Sheer, *Addressing the Problem of Juvenile Bullying,* at
www.justicestudies.com/weblibrary

Read the OJJDP publication, *Juvenile Mentoring Program: A Progress Review,* at
www.justicestudies.com/weblibrary

Visit the Anti-Bullying Network via www.justicestudies.com/webplaces

Visit Bullying.org via www.justicestudies.com/webplaces

Visit the School Safety sections of the National Education Association's web site via
www.justicestudies.com/webplaces

Learn about bullying and what can be done to prevent it from national Youth Violence Prevention Resource Center's web site via www.justicestudies.com/webplaces

www.dropoutprevention.org

www.incacs.org

CHAPTER 10: GANGS AND DELINQUENCY

LEARNING OBJECTIVES

After reading this chapter, you should be able to answer the following questions:

1. What is the relationship between peer groups and gang activity?

2. How have gangs evolved in the United States?

3. What is the relationship between urban-based gangs and emerging gangs and emerging gangs in smaller cities and communities?

4. How extensive is gang activity in this country?

5. How does gang activity affect communities?

6. Why do youths join gangs?

7. How can gangs be prevented and controlled?

CHAPTER SUMMARY

This chapter examines *gangs* and their relationship to delinquent behaviors and other criminal acts. Youngsters derive meaning from social contacts with family members, peers, teachers, and leaders and participants in churches, community organizations and school activities. The socialization of societal values and norms occurs in large part due to both intentional and unintentional agents of our society. As a result of the socialization process, some youngsters find little reason to become involved in law-violating activities. Yet, others with needs often frustrated and nowhere else left to find hope, become attracted to street gangs to fill the physical and emotional voids created by a variety of situations and explanations. In short, gangs become quasi-families and offer acceptance, status, and esteem to children when the soil is fertile for the planting of such seeds.

Youth gangs are proliferating across the United States. Even small towns and rural areas are experiencing a rise in youth gangs and their criminal activities. The advent of gangs in society is not new, however the severity of violence and the methods of inflicting it have changed, especially the use of automatic and semi-automatic weapons by gang members. Drug trafficking has also changed in stature with gangs. What once was a peripheral activity is now a main source of income for many street gangs. Youth gangs have further become street gangs, particularly in urban areas. Juveniles tend to stay with the gang into adulthood and assume more control of gang operations as they age.

Children of the underclass are often susceptible to gang membership due to poverty and conditions associated with urban neighborhoods. Integrated and multidimensional efforts are needed to have any long-term effect on preventing and controlling gangs and their criminal actions.

LECTURE OUTLINE

Introduction

- The case of Walter Simon: Eight shots from a rival gang.
- Social World of the Delinquent: Mara Salvatrucha MS-13

I. Peer Groups and Gangs

A. Peer Groups and Delinquent Behavior
- Conflicting findings within the research, however most agree that delinquency occurs in groups. Shaw and McKay suggested 82 percent. Jensen states juveniles follow *herd instincts* when they violate the law.
- Hirschi refers to peer relations as *cold and brittle*.
- Giordano/Cernkovich found delinquents have *friendship patterns*.
- Warr states delinquent friends tend to be *sticky* friends.
- Debate is largely causal ordered or what comes first, delinquency or peers.

II. The Development of Gangs in the United States
- Gangs have existed since the Revolutionary war. Wild West era with the James/Younger gangs.
- Youth gangs flourished in Chicago and other large cities in nineteenth century.

A. Gangs and Play Activity: The 1920s through 1940s.
- Thrasher viewed gangs as a normal part of ethnic neighborhoods. Largely transitory, organized and protective of turf. Bonded with each other without any sense of particular purpose or goal.

B. West Side Story Era: The 1950s
- Teenage gangs are more established in urban areas. They were violent, but did not have the same weapons of today's gangs.
- Millions of dollars spent to prevent and control the gangs with little or no reduction occurring.

C. Development of the Modern Gang: The 1960s
- Drugs influence gangs for the first time in the midst of rapid social changes. Drugs actually reduced gang activity in some areas due to members being self-absorbed into drugs (out of sight out of mind).
- The emergence also of super-gangs such as Crips, Vice Lords, and Disciples. (see insert 10.1).

- Super-gangs were involved in social and political activism (Operation Bootstrap). After working against Daley's campaign in Chicago, many were sent to prison due to gang crackdowns by law enforcement.

D. Expansion, Violence, and Criminal Operations: the 1970s to the Present
- 1970s and 1980s as gang leadership is assumed by adults, they become more responsible for criminal activities. Some are regarded by law enforcement as organized crime.
- Miller contends that gangs were committing one-third of all violent juvenile crime.
- 1980s crack cocaine was turning point for gangs, some established link to Columbian drug smugglers.
- Gangs are now becoming a worldwide focus in many different countries.

III. The Nature and Extent of Gang Activity
- By 2002 estimated 21,500 gangs are in the United States. This is a decline from 1996.
- 2002 National Youth Gang Survey reveals: Gang activity is down, largest drop in gang membership is suburban areas, most gang members are adult, and most are Hispanic followed by African-American then white and Asian.

A. Definitions of Gangs
- Thrasher's definition in 1927 and Miller's definition in 1970s, suggest a gang is bonded together with mutual interests, identifiable leadership, and other organizational features, to conduct illegal activity and control over territory.
- Esbensen includes ages of 12 to 24, use of colors and a sense of permanence.

B. Profiles of Gang Members
- The smaller the community more likely gang members will be juveniles. Urban gangs tend to have a majority of adult members.
- Younger members tend to run errands and serve as drug runners due to their age.
- *Regulars* are strongly attached to the gang, *peripherals* participate less than regulars and have other interests, *temporaries* are marginally committed, *situational* members participate only in certain activities.
- Reiner identifies; *at-risk* as pre-gang members, *wannabes* are recruits in pre-teen years, *associates* are the lowest level, *hard-core* are regular members, and *veteranos* are the older members.
- Klein and Maxson: traditional gang (20 year existence), neotraditional gang (10 year existence, compressed gang (50 members), collective gang (less developed), and specialty gang (small with narrow focus of activities.
- *People (5 point star) and Folks (6 point star)*: Chicago area beginnings.

C. Gangs in Schools
- School is fertile soil for youth gangs. Members bring guns to school, recruit new members from school, conflict arises at school between rival gangs.
- Schools have an economic base for drug dealing. Drug distribution was so extensive in Dallas, students were required to wear picture ID's.

D. Urban Street Gangs
- Gangs are *quasi-institutionalized.* Students seek protection in gangs.
- Dysfunctional nature of families raises the appeal for gangs. Some gangs take control of schools.
- Vertical/hierarchal gangs (Chicago based gangs).
- Horizontal/commission gangs (Bloods/Crips).
- Influential model gangs (No duties or titles of leadership).
- Gang life can look glamorous to younger recruits.
- Clothing, colors, signing are held as sacred by most gang members (tagging).
- Prayers are rituals in many gangs.
- Loyalty is a chief value in gangs.
- Hispanic gangs and *locura (craziness)* due to presence of fear.
- Gang *migration* occurs three ways: 1) satellite gangs, 2) relocation, and 3) expansion of drug markets (relocation is the most typical pattern).
- Changing structure of economy encourages teen members to continue with gangs into their adult years (loss of jobs).
- Core members are more involved with serious delinquent acts than fringe members. Gang boys persisted nearly three years longer than non-gang boys.
- Rochester study says gangs commit 7 times more delinquency than nongang offenders.
- Studies suggest that gang membership is more influential on youth violence than influence of other delinquent peers.
- Youth gang homicides might be increasing since 1998, according to 2002 NYGS.
- Peaks and valleys of gang violence is related to several factors, gun ownership, and extent of organization into crime groups.

E. Gangs in Small Communities
- No gangs are entirely alike. Expansion began in late 1980s and appeared to be fueled in four ways; expansion of the *crack-cocaine* market into smaller areas, some gang members operating on their own, gang member families that moved to new communities, and independent formation by youths free of outside interventions and constraints.
- Stages include: 1) Implementation, 2) expansion and conflict, 3) organization and consolidation, 4) Gang intimidation and community reaction, 5) expansion of drug markets, 6) gang takeover, and 7) community deterioration.

F. Racial and Ethnic Gangs
- Hispanic and African-American gangs are more numerous, but Asian gangs are rapidly increasing.
- Hispanic gangs are divided into categories with Chicano being most prevalent with codes of *Movidas.* Chicano gangs are very loyal.
- African-American gangs have established drug networks across the nation.
- Asian gangs are largely in California and tend to be more organized than others. Heroin trafficking is characteristic of their economic base.
- White gangs have a propensity to satanic worship and *stoners.* Metal music and outlandish apparel are common. Neo-Nazi groups are involved in hate crimes.

- Native American gangs have centered around Navajo groups involved in drinking.

G. Female Delinquent Gangs
- Female gangs may be independent or have connections to male gangs.
- Most studies suggest female gang activity is lower than males.
- Females are more likely to be involved in property crimes and status offenses.
- Gangs may provide girls with ways to survive in a harsh environment.

IV. Theories of Gang Formation
- Bloch and Niederhoffer suggest joining gangs is part of the male experience to grow up. Gangs provide puberty rites found in other cultures.
- Cloward and Ohlin contend gangs pursue illegitimate means due to being restricted from opportunities to legitimate means to achieve societal goals.
- Miller suggests that gang membership is an expression of lower-class subculture.
- Yablonsky states gangs are created from conditions of urban slums.
- *Underclass theory* states gangs are a natural response to an abnormal social setting.
- Call for an *integrated approach* to understand gang involvement.

A. Gangs Across the Life Course
- Gangs membership is a trajectory for some. Gangs may serve as a turning point.
- Gang membership has an impact on ones' life-course development.

V. Preventing and Controlling Youth Gangs
- Communities have a tendency to deny a gang problem, until a dramatic episode occurs.
- Spergel and colleagues suggest five strategies for gang intervention; *(1) community organization, (2) social intervention, (3) opportunities provision, (4) suppression, and (5) creation of special organizational units.*
- Mobilization of school officials, employers, street workers, police, judges, prosecutors, and probation/parole/correctional officers. Community-wide approach.
- Integrated, multidimensional, community oriented effort is likely to have long-term effects in preventing and controlling gangs.

KEY TERMS

cold and brittle Hirschi's term to describe interpersonal relationships between delinquents.

crack Controlled substance derived from cocaine that is usually smoked and is cheaper to produce than conventional cocaine, therefore becoming attractive to gangs for marketing.

emerging gangs Gang formation occurring within smaller communities, which began in the 1980s with the expansions of drug trafficking into smaller cities and promises of satellite operations connected to larger urban gangs.

friendship patterns   The nature of the peer relationships that exist within a teenage culture.

gang   A group of youths who are bound together by mutual interests, have identifiable leadership, and act in concert to achieve a specific purpose that generally includes the conduct of illegal activity.

locura   State of mind associated with Mexican-American street gangs denoting craziness or wildness.

movidas   Codes of moral honor and conduct followed by Chicano gangs.

People and Folks   During the 1970's the gangs within the Illinois prison system divided themselves up into two categories: the People and the Folks. Some of the gangs were identified as "people" gangs and other gangs were identified as "folk" gangs.

representing   Displays by gang affiliates in which a hand sign, colors, articles of clothing, or other objects are used to represent and symbolize affiliation with particular gang membership.

Practice Test

Multiple Choice:

1. The vignette at the beginning of the chapter began with a story about Walter Simon. He is mentioned in the text because _____.
a. he was murdered by gang members
b. as a gang member he murdered 3 people
c. he started the Gangster Disciples
d. he was shot 8 times in San Francisco
e. he was a San Francisco police officer who was murdered by a Latino Gang.

2. Over the last 30 years, urban street gangs have armed themselves with _____.
a. Israeli made Uzis
b. Soviet AK-47's
c. American M-16's
d. All of the above

3. *Mara* is a Salvadorian word for _____.
a. criminal
b. crime
c. gang
d. man
e. macho

4. The gang Mara Salvatrucha is from _____.
a. El Salvador
b. Mexico
c. Nicaragua
d. Costa Rica
e. Columbia

5. Mara Salvatrucha is also known as _____.
a. Mara Salvatrucha 13
b. MS-13
c. MS XIII
d. All of the above

6. In gang language the number 13 refers to _____.
a. the original 13 leaders of the Gangster Disciples
b. the unluckiness of gang members
c. 13th letter of the alphabet which is M
d. the age at which a juvenile becomes eligible to join a gang
e. All of the above

7. Research by Clifford R. Shaw and Henry D. McKay showed that _____.
a. the majority of crimes committed by juveniles are committed as lone individuals
b. the majority of crimes committed by juveniles are committed in groups
c. juveniles, in fact, rarely commit crimes
d. the majority of murders in America are committed by gang members
e. the majority of rapes in America are committed by gang members

8. Which of the following officers referred to gang relationships as being "cold and brittle".
a. Clifford R. Shaw and Henry D. McKay
b. Edwin Sutherland
c. Travis Hirschi
d. George Knox
e. Frederick Thrasher

9. Who is the author of the famous book *The Gang: A Study of 1,313 Gangs in Chicago*?
a. Clifford R. Shaw and Henry D. McKay
b. Edwin Sutherland
c. Travis Hirschi
d. George Knox
e. Frederick Thrasher

10. The musical *West Side Story* was about two gangs. Their names were _____.
a. the Crips and the Bloods
b. the Vice Lords and the Gangster Disciples
c. the Shamrocks and the PR's
d. the Sharks and the Jets
e. Folks and People

11. In the 1960's, the Crips began in the city of _____.
a. New York
b. Los Angeles
c. Chicago
d. Detroit
e. Houston

12. Which of the following gangs began in Chicago?
a. Vice Lords
b. Black Stone Rangers
c. Gangster Disciples
d. All of the above

13. Who is the leader of the Gangster Disciples?
a. Larry Hoover
b. Jeff Fort
c. Joe Rossi
d. Willie Lloyd
e. Tu Pac

14. Who was one of the leaders of the Almighty Vice Lord Nation?
a. Larry Hoover
b. Jeff Fort
c. Joe Rossi
d. Willie Lloyd
e. Tu Pac

15. Who was the leader of the Black Stone Nation?
a. Larry Hoover
b. Jeff Fort
c. Joe Rossi
d. Willie Lloyd
e. Tu Pac

16. According to the *2004 National Youth Gang Survey* there are an estimated _____ gang members in the United States.
a. 760,000
b. 500,000
c. 400,000
d. 250,000
e. 130,000

17. According to the *2004 National Youth Gang Survey* there are an estimated _____ gangs in the United States.
a. 52,000
b. 24,000
c. 17,000
d. 13,000
e. 10,000

18. Richard A. Cloward and Lloyd E. Ohlin identified 3 different types of gangs. Which of the following is not one of those types?
a. Drug Gangs
b. Criminal Gangs
c. Conflict Gangs
d. Retreatist Gangs

19. C. Ronald Huff's examination of gangs in Cleveland and Columbus identified 3 basic groups. Which of the following is not one of those groups.
a. Drug Gangs
b. Informal Hedonistic Gangs
c. Instrumental Gangs
d. Predatory Gangs

20. The general classification of gangs as People or Folks is best characteristic of which city?
a. New York
b. Chicago
c. Los Angeles
d. London
e. Beijing

21. Martin Jankowski observed 3 types of gang organizational structures. Which of the following is not one of those structures?
a. The vertical/hierachical type
b. The horizontal/commission type
c. The influential model
d. The totalitarian model

22. Martin Jankowski points out that there are 3 basic recruitment strategies the gangs use in soliciting new members. Which of the following is not one of those techniques?
a. Fraternity type of recruitment
b. Obligation type of recruitment
c. Loyalty type of recruitment
d. Coercive type if recruitment

23. When a new male member of a gang must fight other members as part of his initiation is it called _____.
a. Blessed-In
b. Jumped-In
c. Sexed-In
d. Blood-In
e. All of the above

24. When a new member of a gang has relatives who are already in the gang, he may be
_____.
a. Blessed-In
b. Jumped-In
c. Sexed-In
d. Blood-In
e. All of the above

25. The major reasons for gang members remaining in the gang into their adult years is
_____.
a. the changing structure of the economy
b. the loss of unskilled of skilled and semi-skilled jobs
c. the lucrative drug markets
d. all of the above

True/False:

1. The gang MS-13 is known solely for drug sells and is not a very violent gang.

2. One of the strongest findings of criminology, according to Ross L. Matsueda and Kathleen Anderson, "is that delinquent behavior is correlated with delinquency of one's peers."

3. Researchers generally agree that most delinquent behavior is committed by individuals not groups.

4. Offenders who are 13 and under are more likely to commit crimes in pairs and groups than are 16 and 17 year old offenders.

5. Frederick Thrasher viewed gangs as a normal part of growing up in ethnic neighborhoods.

6. The majority of all gang members are 17 or younger.

7. The majority of all gang members are now females instead of males.

8. When the Chicago Crime Commission studied the websites of several Chicago Area gangs, they found that Amazon.com was advertising on gang websites.

9. Some officers have found gang websites useful in prosecuting gang members.

10. When a gang member is convicted of a crime, it is against the law to give him a longer prison sentence simply because he is a member of a gang.

Fill-in-the-blank:

1. In your book, the way Hirschi's described interpersonal relationships between delinquents was _____.

2. A controlled substance derived from cocaine that is usually smoked, cheaper to produce than conventional cocaine, and attractive for gangs to marketing is known as _____.

3. _____ was a problem that occurred within smaller communities beginning in the 1980s with the expansions of drug trafficking and the promise of satellite connections to larger urban gangs.

4. The nature of the peer relationships that exist within a teenage culture is called _____.

5. A group of youths who are bound together by mutual interests, identifiable leadership, and act in concert to achieve a specific illegal activity are commonly called a _____.

6. A state of mind associated with Mexican-American street gangs denoting craziness or wildness is called _____.

7. The codes of moral honor and conduct followed by Chicano gangs is called

_____

8. During the 1970's the gangs within the Illinois prison system divided themselves into two categories, the _____.

9. Displays by gang affiliates, or _____, where hand signs, colors, clothing, or other objects are used to represent and symbolize affiliation with particular gang membership.

Essay:

1. What are the six major elements most frequently cited in the definition of a gang?

2. Frederick Thrasher, in 1927, was one of the first to attempt to define a youth gang. State clearly and completely his definition of a youth gang.

3. Finn-Aage Esbensan concluded that there had to be five elements present for a group to be classified as a youth gang. What are those five elements?

4. J.D. Vigil and J.M. Long identified four basic types of gang involvement explain each of these types.

5. Ira Reiner identified five different types of gang members based on their commitment to the gang. Explain those different types of gang members.

6. In probably the most comprehensive classification of gangs, Malcolm W. Cline and Sheryl l. Maxson distinguished among 5 types of street gangs. Explain each of those types.

7. Martin Jankowski points out that there are 3 basic recruitment strategies used by the gangs. Briefly explain each of these strategies.

8. What are the different methods of initiation into a gang?

Multiple Choice:
1. Answer: d   2. Answer: d   3. Answer: c   4. Answer: a   5. Answer: d   6. Answer: c
7. Answer: b   8. Answer: c   9. Answer: e   10. Answer: d   11. Answer: b   12. Answer: d
13. Answer: a   14. Answer: d   15. Answer: b   16. Answer: a   17. Answer: b
18. Answer: a   19. Answer: a   20. Answer: b   21. Answer: d   22. Answer: c
23. Answer: b   24. Answer: a   25. Answer: d

True/False:
1. False 2. True   3. False   4. True   5. True   6. False   7. False   8. True   9. True
10. False

Fill-in-the-blank:
1. cold and brittle
2. crack
3. Emerging gangs
4. friendship patterns
5. gang
6. locura
7. movidas
8. People and Folks
9. representing

WEBSITES

Read the OJJDP publication, *Co-Offending and Patterns of Juvenile Crime,* at
www.justicestudies.com/weblibrary

Read the OJJDP Fact Sheet, *Highlights of the 2002-2003 National Gang Surveys.* at
www.justicestudies.com/weblibrary

Read the COPS publication, *Solutions to Address Gang Crime,* at
www.justicestudies.com/weblibrary

Visit the National Youth Gang Center's Web site via www.justicestudies.com/webplaces

Visit the National Gang Crime Research Center's Web site via
www.justicestudies.com/webplaces

Read Mike Carlie's, *Into the Abyss: A Personal Journey Into the World of Street Gangs* at
www.justicestudies.com/webplaces

www.streetgangs.com

www.criminology.fsu.edu/jjclearinghouse/jj13.html

CHAPTER 11: DRUGS AND DELINQUENCY

LEARNING OBJECTIVES

After you read this chapter, you should be able to answer the following questions:

1. How are social attitudes related to drug use?

2. How much drug use is there among adolescents in American society?

3. What are the main types of drugs used by adolescents?

4. What is the relationship between drug abuse and delinquency?

5. What theoretical explanations best explain the onset of drug use?

6. What can be done to prevent and control drug use among adolescents?

CHAPTER SUMMARY

This chapter examines the use of drugs and alcohol among adolescents in the United States and its relationship to delinquency. A number of theories have been proposed for the onset and escalation of adolescent drug use. Economic situation, peer influence, addict prone personality, high or peak experience, and sociological origins have all been used to explain the appeal of substance abuse. Bartollas contends that integrated approaches make to most sense in developing an understanding of both drug use and abuse.

Trends in drug use have shown a significant decline from the late 1970s, with perhaps only slight increases occurring since the early 1990s with certain types of drugs. Alcohol continues to be the most abused substance by adolescents, followed by cigarettes, and marijuana topping the list of illicit drugs. The rate of illicit drug use is higher among those using cigarettes and alcohol. While the rate of marijuana use has gone up sharply since 1997, it still has not topped the levels reached in 1979. Studies indicate that fewer adolescents are experimenting with drugs and the heavy drug users tend to be white males. Illicit drug usage is more common on the East and West coasts and less common in the South. Low achievers in school are more susceptible to drug usage than high achievers. Ecstasy (MDMA) became widely used in the 1990s along with Crank (methamphetamine) which some had predicted would set off a new drug epidemic in the 1990s. Bartollas suggests it never fully materialized and federal efforts to control drug usage by declaring war have largely failed.

While the rate of drug usage is still considered high in this nation, it is especially high among high-risk children. Early prevention efforts in school, as well as in other social contexts, appear to be making headway with low-risk children. However, prevention, treatment, or punishment does not appear to be reducing the amount or seriousness of substance abuse with high-risk children. Research contends that social influence and peer interventions were found to have the most lasting effect on prevention and reduction of drug usage in the United States.

LECTURE OUTLINE

Introduction
- Simon Curtis: The story of a graffiti artist.

I. Drug Use Among Adolescents
- Alcohol remains the substance of choice for most adolescents.
- Drug use peaked in1979 and has declined significantly since 2001.
- Marijuana and cocaine use declined since 1999.
- Cigarette use peaked in 1974 and Inhalant use peaked in 1985.
- High school females are more likely to smoke than high school males.
- Males are more likely to be involved in heavy binge drinking than females.
- Substance abuse is higher on the East and West coasts and lowest in the South.

II. Types of Drugs

A. What's in a Name?
- Brand Name
- Generic Name
- Street Name
- Psychoactive Category

B. Alcohol and Tobacco
- Reaction to *Prohibition* fostered the view that alcohol is acceptable.
- Tobacco is often neglected in discussions on drugs, however more deaths are attributed to tobacco than alcohol and illicit drugs combined.

C. Marijuana
- Most frequently used illicit drug. Research indicates more ill effects of long-term use than believed in the past.

D. Cocaine
- Derivative of the coca plant, once believed to be less addicting than other hard drugs.
- Snorting is most common, however *freebasing* (smoking) was popular in 1980s. Intravenous use (*speedballing*) is dangerous and killed John Belushi in 1982.
- *Crack* is a more potent, less expensive refinement of cocaine (usually smoked) that arrived in the inner-cities in the early 1980s.
- *Crack* addicted *babies* are the consequences of adolescent addiction.

E. Methamphetamine
- Synthetic drug (crank, ice, chalk, glass, and crystal).
- The use of methamphetamine is growing.

F. Inhalants
- *Butyl nitrite* commonly called *RUSH,* is probably most frequently used. Others include vapors from gasoline, paint thinners, glue, and aerosol cans.

G. Sedatives
- Barbiturates used to depress the nervous system. Includes *Quaaludes, Amytals,* and *Tuinals, Valium, Librium, Equanil (Benzodiazepines).*

H. Amphetamines
- Used in WWII by Americans (*Benzedrine, Dexedrine*) used by truckers and people wanting to lose weight.
- 1990s *Ecstasy* (MDMA) became popular. Normally tablets are ingested, but it can be snorted and smoked. Originally used by psychiatrists until outlawed in 1986.

I. Hallucinogens
- Mind altering drugs popular in the 1960s include LSD, PCP and 1970s. Popularity dropped after 1980 to a low of less than 3 percent by 1990 after public hysteria over dangers of hallucinogens.

K. Heroin
- Derivative of opium introduced at turn of the twentieth century. Known as: horse, shit, smack, H, harry, henry, boy, and brown.

L Anabolic Steroids
- There are 100 different types of anabolic steroids. Street names include "Arnolds", Gym Candy", "Juice", "Pampers", "Stackers", and "Weight Trainers".

M Delinquency in America
- Prescription drugs find a place in teen culture.

III. Drug Use and Delinquency
- Issue under debate is whether drugs cause delinquency or does delinquency lead to drug use.
- Considered an overlapping and interrelated problem. (Jessor's Model) Three variables: the personality system, environment system, and the behavior system.
- Abuse is related to delinquency in youth (Denver, Pittsburgh, Rochester studies).
- Widespread support for a sequential pattern of involvement in drug use during adolescence. Alcohol, to marijuana, to other drugs. Some youths experiment then discontinue, others continue into adulthood (without major interference) and some become addicted to the point their lives revolve around drugs.
- Family history, early antisocial behavior and academic failure contribute to drug use.
- Nearly 50 percent of serious juvenile offenders are multiple drug users, alcohol usage is four to nine times greater than for nonoffenders, and marijuana use is fourteen times more likely by serious offenders compared to nonoffenders.

A. Drug-Trafficking Juveniles

- Some researchers have suggested that *crack* distribution is not a street gang phenomenon. Suburbs and schools are generally serviced by independent juveniles.
- Urban settings are largely serviced by adults, not juveniles. Chicago study revealed most juveniles barely make survival income from drug deals.

B. Drug Use Through the Life Course

- Two basic pathways, (1) abusers may not be involved with delinquency, and (2) abusers participating in other delinquent acts.
- About two-thirds of abusers continue to abuse drugs into adulthood but about half desist from other forms of criminality.
- Alcohol and drug use increases the risk of youth pregnancies, early parenthood, dropping out of school, and premature independent living from parents.
- Substance abuse affects adolescent development.
- *Relapse* is attributed to those who do not find the straight life fulfilling.
- Principle Reports that drug testing students works.

IV. Explaining the Onset of Drug Abuse

- Determining whether it is the onset of drug abuse.
- No single comprehensive picture of what causes adolescents' use of drugs
- Cognitive-Affective Theories
- Addictive Personality Theories
- Stress Relief Theories
- Social Learning Theories
- Social Control Theories
- Social Disorganization Theories
- Integrated Theories

V. Solving the Drug Problem

A. Prevention

- Tobler's meta-analysis of prevention programs; (1) knowledge oriented (education), (2) affective strategies (psychological) only, (3) social influence and life skills (peer pressure), (4) knowledge plus affective (attitude and values altered), and (5) alternative strategies (school).
- Tobler concluded that social influence and peer interventions have the most lasting effects.
- Effective programs include: early childhood and family interventions, school-based interventions, and comprehensive community-wide efforts.

B. Treatment Intervention

- Treatment takes place in hospitals for those who can afford it. Others utilize privately administered placements, which vary greatly. Serious delinquents will likely be placed in state facilities whose basic goals are security-oriented.
- No real evidence that juvenile treatment is any more successful than adults.
- Willingness to change may be related to success of some intervention programs.

KEY TERMS

alcohol   Considered the most abused substance by adolescents due to the perception that it is not socially unacceptable compared to illicit drugs. Perceptions of alcohol were largely affected by historical significance of Prohibition.

amphetamines   A controlled substance largely used by Americans after WWII. Normally ingested in pill or capsule form and known as *uppers* such as Benzedrine and Dexedrine. Ecstasy and methamphetamine are newer forms of amphetamine that were popularized in the 1990s.

club drug   A synthetic psychoactive substance often found at nightclubs, bars, "raves", and dance parties. Club drugs include MDMA (Ecstasy), ketamine, methamphetamine (meth), GBL, PCP, GHB, and Rohpnol.

cocaine   Derived from coca plants and originally used as a painkiller. Typically snorted, and decreased in popularity after the 1980s due to the high cost, and the advent of cocaine's alternative derivative of *crack,* which is cheaper and more potent.

heroin   Derivative of morphine which is extracted from the opiate base of poppies. Normally injected intravenously. Highly addictive and experienced resurgence in the 1990s with juveniles.

inhalants   Variety of substances that are *huffed* or snorted which produce disorientation and perceived euphoria. Substances inhaled include glue, paint thinners, aerosol cans, and butyl nitrite.

marijuana   The most abused illicit drug by juveniles. Plant material, which contains natural chemical amounts of THC producing mild euphoria and is usually smoked. Sometimes referred to as the *gateway* drug meaning it will lead to harder forms of drug abuse.

sedatives   Barbiturates drugs intended to reduce the metabolic rate and commonly known as *downers*, such as Quaaludes. Frequently used in combination with *uppers* to establish a dosage baseline.

PRACTICE TEST

Multiple Choice:

1. The vignette at the beginning of the chapter involved the IRAK crew who were known for
_____.
   a. selling drugs
   b. committing a murder
   c. being graffiti artists
   d. stealing computers from their school
   e. terrorism

2. The drug of choice for most adolescents is _____.
   a. cocaine
   b. heroin
   c. marijuana
   d. crack
   e. alcohol

3. Drug use since 2001 can be characterized as _____.
   a. increasing 10% per year
   b. increasing 5% per year
   c. a slight downturn in drug use levels
   d. a significant downturn in drug use levels

4. What percent of high school students use marijuana sometime during their life?
   a. 10%
   b. 20%
   c. 30%
   d. 40%
   e. 50%

5. Which of the following has the lowest use of illicit drugs?
   a. whites
   b. blacks
   c. Latino
   d. Asians

6. A craving for a particular drug, accompanied by physical dependence, which motivates continuing usage, resulting in tolerance of the drugs effects is called _____.
a. cracking
b. strung out
c. drug addiction
d. bad habit

7. The name that a manufacture gives a chemical substance is its _____.
a. brand name
b. generic name
c. street name
d. psychoactive category

8. PCP and angel dust are _____.
a. brand name
b. generic name
c. street name
d. psychoactive category

9. The other name for marijuana is _____.
a. Acapulco gold
b. African black
c. Columbian gold
d. Giggle weed
e. all of the above

10. The major source of cocaine is _____.
a. Mexico
b. Iraq
c. Afghanistan
d. Ecuador
e. Columbia

11. Another name for cocaine is _____.
a. coke
b. nose candy
c. toot
d. Super Fly
e. all of the above

12. MADD is an organization that attacks _____.
a. the use of marijuana
b. the use of cocaine
c. drunk driving
d. the existence of gangs
e. all of the above

13. John Belushi died in 1982 from _____.
a. drunk driving
b. heroin
c. crack
d. speed-balling
e. methamphetamines

14. Methamphetamine is a _____.
a. drug made from opium
b. drug made from heroin
c. drug made from cocaine
d. a synthetic drug

15. The term RUSH is used to describe _____.
a. inhalants
b. sedatives
c. methamphetamine
d. heroin
e. coke

16. Sedatives have a common factor in that they are _____.
a. smoked
b. taken orally
c. shot up
d. sniffed
e. none of the above

17. It is difficult to manufacture meth in New England because _____.
a. the ingredients are not native to New England
b. meth smells so bad that you need wide open spaces to produce it
c. organized crime is opposed to the use of meth
d. the winters are too cold

18. The common name for MDMA is _____.
a. ecstasy
b. mushrooms
c. amphetamines
d. marijuana
e. crack

19. The source of heroin is _____.
a. cocaine
b. amphetamines
c. meth
d. opium

20. This particular type of drug can be rubbed on the skin in the form of creams or gels.
a. anabolic steroids
b. cocaine
c. heroin
d. amphetamines

21. One of the newest patterns of drug usage is called a "pharm party'. A "pharm party" is

_____.
a. a keg party on a farm
b. a party where a pig is roasted
c. a fraternity party
d. a party where teens exchange pharmaceutical drugs

22. In 2005, what percentage of U.S. teenagers said they had used prescription pain killers such as Vicodin or stimulants such as Ritalin to get high?
a. 9%
b. 19%
c. 29%
d. 39%

23. Schools may test teenagers for drug usage. What percentage of schools have drug testing policies?
a. 2%
b. 8%
c. 12%
d. 18%
e. 25%

24. What is the strongest predictor of an individuals involvement in drug use?
a. the students grade point average in school
b. parents income
c. drug use by peers
d. the students race

25. Heroin is also called _____.
a. horse
b. speed-balling
c. amphetamines
d. anabolic steroids

True/False:

1. Drug and alcohol use and juvenile delinquency have been identified as the most serious problem behaviors of adolescents.

2. In the last few years there has been a declined in drug use by adolescents.

3. During the Bush Administration, the use of drugs has significantly increased.

4. The rates of illicit drug use in 2002 were about the same for white, African American, and Hispanic/Latino youth.

5. Heavy drinking is more prevalent among African American youths than it is among white youths.

6. Smoking continues to be a problem and has increased 12% with 8th graders.

7. The use of crack during pregnancy contributes to the premature separation of the placenta from the uterus, which results in stillbirths and premature infants.

8. Considerable research has found that delinquency tends to follow the onset of drug usage.

9. Young abusers of prescription drugs have been using the internet to share "recipes" for getting high.

10. The Supreme Court has ruled that a students right to privacy is more important than a schools right to know if they are using drugs.

11. One reason many drug addicts relapse is that they do not find the straight life sufficiently exciting, fulfilling, or satisfying.

12. The War on Drugs has not been won with juveniles anymore than it has with adults.

Fill-in-the-Blank:

1. A drug made through a fermentation process that relaxes inhibitions and causes adolescents to participate in risky behavior while under its influence is called _____.

2. Stimulant drugs that occur in various forms and are frequently used by adolescents are called _____.

3. A synthetic psychoactive substance often found at nightclubs, bars, "raves," and dance parties is called _____.

4. A coca extract that creates mood elevation, elation, grandiose feelings, and feelings of heightened physical prowess is _____.

5. The excessive use of a drug, which is frequently characterized by physical and/or psychological dependence is called _____.

6. A form of amphetamine that began to be used by adolescents (for sexual enhancement) in the United States in the 1980s and 1990s and is now rather widespread is _____.

7. A refined form of morphine that was introduced around the beginning of the twentieth century is _____.

8. Volatile liquids that give off a vapor, which is inhaled, producing short-term excitement and euphoria followed by a period of disorientation is called a _____

9. The most frequently used illicit drug is _____. It is usually smoked and consists of dried hemp leaves and buds.

10. Drugs that are taken orally and affect the user by depressing the nervous system causing drowsiness are called _____.

Essay:

1. Explain the cognitive-affective theory of drug usage.

2. Explain the addictive personality theory of drug usage.

3. Explain the stress relief theory of drug usage.

4. What is the social learning theory of drug usage?

5. Explain Travis Hirschi's social control theory and its relationship to explaining drug usage.

6. Explain how drug courts work.

Multiple Choice:
1. Answer: c   2. Answer: e   3. Answer: d   4. Answer: d   5. Answer: d   6. Answer: c
7. Answer: a   8. Answer: c   9. Answer: e   10. Answer: e   11. Answer: e   12. Answer: c
13. Answer: d   14. Answer: d   15. Answer: a   16. Answer: b   17. Answer: b
18. Answer: a   19. Answer: d   20. Answer: a   21. Answer: d   22. Answer: b
23. Answer: a   24. Answer: c   25. Answer: a

True/False:
1. True 2. True   3. False   4. True   5. False   6. False   7. True   8. False   9. True
10. False   11. True   12. True

Fill-in-the-blank:
1. alcohol
2. amphetamines
3. club drugs
4. cocaine
5. drug addiction
6. ecstacy
7. heroin
8. inhalants
9. marijuana
10. sedatives

WEBSITES

Read the COPS publication, *Underage Drinking,* at
www.justicestudies.com/weblibrary

Read the OJJDP Fact Sheet, *Substance Abuse: The Nation's Number One Health Problem,* at
www.justicestudies.com/weblibrary

Read the OJJDP Fact Sheet, *Assessing Alcohol, Drug, and Mental Disorders in Juvenile Detainees,* at www.justicestudies.com/weblibrary

Read the National Drug Intelligence Center *National Drug Threat Assessment* at
www.justicestudies.com/weblibrary

Read the federal *General Counterdrug Intelligence Plan* at
www.justicestudies.com/weblibrary

Read Key Findings from the National Institute on Drug Abuse's Monitoring the Future Survey at
www.justicestudies.com/weblibrary

Read the Office of National Drug Control Policy's *National Drug Control Strategy 2006* at
www.justicestudies.com/weblibrary

Visit the Mothers Against Drunk Driving's Web site via
www.justicestudies.com/webplaces

Visit the National Clearinghouse for Alcohol and Drub Information's Web site via
www.justicestudies.com/webplaces

Visit the Office of National Drub Control Policy's Web site via
www.justicestudies.com/webplaces

Visit the Underage Drinking Enforcement Training Center's Web site via
www.justicestudies.com/webplaces

Visit Clubdrugs.org via www.justicestudies.com/webplaces

Visit the drub Enforcement Administration's (DEA) Web site via
www.justicestudies.com/webplaces

Visit the National Drug Intelligence Center's Web site via www.justicestudies.com/webplaces

www.lec.org/DrugSearch/Documents/Amphetamines.html

www.virlib.ncjrs.org/DrugsAndCrime.asp

CHAPTER 12: PREVENTION, DIVERSION, AND TREATMENT

LEARNING OBJECTIVES

After reading this chapter your should be able to answer the following questions:

1. What type of prevention programs are likely to work with high-risk youngsters?

2. What ate the advantages and disadvantages of the diversionary programs?

3. What treatment modalities are most widely used with juvenile delinquents?

4. What are the common characteristics of effective programs?

CHAPTER SUMMARY

Delinquency prevention programs have generally fallen short of controlling youth crime. Grass-roots community groups appear to offer the most promising approach of the various prevention programs of the twentieth century in preventing delinquency. For delinquency prevention programs to have significant success in preventing youth crime, it will be necessary to modify the social, economic, and political conditions of American society. *Primary* and *secondary prevention* programs have been barely adequate at delinquency prevention to date.

Diversion programs have evolved mainly from programs initiated by police, probation officers, the juvenile court, and other outside the system agencies. Most of the programs of the 1960s and 1970s were viewed as panaceas for reducing youth crime. The main criticism of diversion programs has been the charge of *net-widening*, in that youths are brought into the system that might not have been otherwise.
Additionally, critics charge that youth prevention programs are considered too expensive. Newly developed *drug* and *teen courts* are recent attempts in the prevention of delinquency. However, it is too soon to analyze their effectiveness.

Much of the research in juvenile delinquency contends that violent and inhumane training schools are among the least promising places for treatment and prevention to occur. Community-based programs traditionally lack resources, which probably helped result in more failures than successes. The 60 Minutes revelation by Robert Martinson, led to a premature and mostly inaccurate perceptions of community-based treatment modalities. Later, meta-analysis revealed reduction in recidivism rates of 10 to 12 percent.

Guided group interaction and *reality therapy* have been used more than most other treatment modalities in treating youth offenders. Both are aimed at making the offender responsible for their actions and teaching a more positive pro-social stance. The *errors in thinking approach*, is a cognitive restructuring strategy that was widely adopted in the 1990s throughout the nation. Program designs have often relied on a single cure for complex problems, lacked integrity, and been inadequate. However, as Bartollas indicates, correctional treatment could work if amenable offenders were offered appropriate treatments.

LECTURE OUTLINE

Introduction
- Karl gets a break. Privately run drug treatment center.

I. Delinquency Prevention
- Emphasis on prevention was incorporated into several federal laws in the 1970s and 1980s.
- Prevention still has largely been ignored.
- *Primary prevention* is focused on modifying physical and social environments.
- *Secondary prevention* refers to intervention programs and is diversionary.
- *Tertiary prevention* is directed at prevention of recidivism (traditional rehabilitation).

A. A History of Well Meant Intentions
- *Panaceas* stem from tendency to seek easy answers and divert attentions away from long-term comprehensive help.
- Panaceas have ranged from biological, psychological, group therapy, gang intervention, recreational activities, job training/employment, and community organization.
- Studies have suggested the effectiveness of these programs is weak.
- Criticized for widening the nets of social control over children, being too expensive, providing piecemeal solutions, and compromising the rights of children.
- In 1990 the Office of Juvenile Justice and Delinquency Prevention began to target the prevention of serious delinquency through reducing chronic delinquency.

B. Comprehensive Strategy for Delinquency Prevention
- First developed in 1980s, a comprehensive framework is made up of typologies of cause focused strategies and awareness of components of programs that work.
- The National Center for the Assessment of Delinquent Behavior and its Prevention suggest three principles: (1) *focus on the causes of delinquency*, (2) *there are multiple causes and correlates of delinquency*, and (3) *experiences during social development*.

C. Promising Prevention Programs
- Public Health Model of Crime Prevention
- The Office of Juvenile Justice and Delinquency Prevention guide (MPG)
- Big Brothers Big Sisters of America (mentoring programs)
- Bully Prevention Program (school programs)
- Functional Family Therapy (intervention program)
- Incredible Years (parent and teacher program to treat conduct problems)
- Life Skills Training (intervention curriculum)
- Midwestern Prevention Project (school-based intervention)
- Multidimensional Treatment Foster Care (short term therapeutic care)
- Multisystematic Therapy (community-based clinical treatment for chronic offenders)

- Nurse-Family Partner ship (prenatal care)
- Project Towards No Drug Abuse (targets high-school youth)
- Promoting Alternative Thinking Strategies (PATH) (teachers and counselors)

D. Programs That Work
- Dryfoos identified; individual counseling and mentoring for high-risk children, multiagency collaborative approach, early identification and intervention, programs located outside of the school, training of staff, providing of coping skills, and using older peer influence for learning.

E. Comprehensive Delinquency Prevention
- Research indicates that high-risk youth can be impacted by well-equipped prevention and treatment programs.
- The comprehensive or multi-systematic: builds on the youth's strengths, operate outside the formal justice system and combines accountability with intensive rehabilitation.

II. How Diversion Works
- Began in 1967 after President's Commission on Law Enforcement, recommended alternatives to the juvenile system based on labeling perspective and differential association theories.

A. Traditional Forms of Diversion
- Belief that diversion would lead to more effective and humane justice.
- Diversion can come from police, courts or agencies outside of the justice system.

B. New Forms of Diversion
- 1990s brought *community courts* with emphasis on restoration, *alternative dispute resolution*(family and victim meetings), *gun courts*(intense intervention related to weapons), *teen courts* (Adult judge-Youth judge-Tribunal-Peer Jury), and drug courts (deferred prosecution for drug treatment).
- Most teen courts receive less than 100 referrals per year. Handle first time offenders and rarely or never accept youths with prior arrest records.
- *Drug courts* established by Title V of the Violent Crime Control and Law Enforcement Act of 1994. More comprehensive intake assessments, focus on the family, coordination of school, community and the juvenile, continual supervision, and application of immediate sanctions.
- Recent studies suggest effects of drug courts may be more stigmatizing than conventional courts for teens.

III. The Treatment Debate
- Correctional treatment came under increased criticism in the late 1960s and 1970s.
- Robert Martinson's 1974 statement was translated as *"nothing works"* by media.
- General mood in the 1980s was one of pessimism and discouragement.

- *Meta-analysis* of treatment programs reveals treatment leads to reduction in recidivism rates.

IV. Most Frequently Used Treatment Modalities

- Modalities used in community-based corrections and training schools include; *psychotherapy, transactional analysis, reality therapy, behavior modification, family therapy, guided group interaction*, and *positive peer culture.*

A. Psychotherapy

- Adaptations of Freudian theory in which offenders are encouraged to talk about past conflicts in individual or group settings. The modality is used more with upper- and middle-class youths and most psychotherapies are conducted in outside agencies.

B. Transactional Analysis

- Focuses on interpreting interpersonal relationships by teaching offenders to relate to problems in a mature manner. Meaning is attached to *"tapes"* of the past and the goal is for offenders to negotiate their own treatment contract.

C. Reality Therapy

- Modality assumes irresponsible behavior occurs when unmet basic needs occur. Uses the three R's; *reality, responsibility, right-and-wrong.*

D. Behavior Modification

- Based on assumption of learning and that behavior is under the control of external environment. Positive reinforcement should encourage good behavior. Some charge the treatment is not long lasting.

E. Guided Group Interaction

- Residential treatment oriented. Assumes confrontation by peers will cause offenders to face the reality of their behaviors. Decision-making is done by the group. Urges the group to be open and honest with each other.

F. Positive Peer Culture

- Teaches group members to care for one another and mobilize the group in positive ways. When caring becomes fashionable, hurting goes out of style.

G. Rational Emotive Therapy

- Rationale is to identify the errors of an offenders thinking such as blaming others, manipulation, and failure to accept obligations. *Cognitive restructuring* of dysfunctional patterns. Widely adopted during the 1990s throughout the nation.

H. Drug and Alcohol Abuse Interventions

- Offenders may be placed in special cottages with specialized staff to lead groups. Outside groups, such as AA or NA make presentations to the group.
- Drug/alcohol problems represent one of the greatest challenges for juvenile justice.

V. What Works for Whom and in What Context
- Some treatment programs have actually made rehabilitation worse. Program designs may have failed to consider what realistically can be accomplished.
- Frequently programs try to apply a single cure for complex problems and lack integrity.
- Correctional treatment could work if amenable offenders are offered appropriate treatments, such as *template-matching* techniques.

KEY TERMS

behavior modification   This modality rewards appropriate behavior positively, immediately, and systematically, and it assumes that rewards increase the occurrence of desired behaviors.

diversion programs   Programs designed outside the formal juvenile justice system to provide alternatives for disposition of juvenile offenders. Programs are aimed at prevention and treatment of youthful offenders.

drug and alcohol abuse interventions   Juvenile offenders may be housed in special cottages with adult team leaders. Outside groups such as Alcoholics Anonymous and Narcotics Anonymous may make presentations to the cottage group.

guided group interaction   Places youthful offenders in a group setting under the direction of adult leaders. Groups often make decisions when an offender will be released or furloughed.

juvenile drug courts   Community court model established by Title V of the 1994 Violent Crime Control and Law Enforcement Act, in which more focus is placed on the family, school and the juvenile offender with immediate sanctions. Typically offers deferred prosecutions in exchange for drug treatment.

panaceas   Quick and generally inadequate remedies for complex problems. Typically panaceas take a piecemeal approach to satisfy public perceptions about juvenile justice problems and solutions.

positive peer culture   Derived from guided group interaction, this approach utilizes positive measures to teach caring principles on the assumption that when caring becomes fashionable, hurting will go out of style.

primary prevention   Prevention strategies based on the modification of an offender's physical and social environments in order to enact changes in his or her behavior and assumingly create rehabilitation.

psychotherapy   Developed by Freud and assumes that talking about one's behavior and feelings of past conflicts will lead to release of emotions. Sessions are conducted in group or individually and are typically reserved more for the upper-and middle-class offenders.

rational emotive therapy   Yochelson and Samenow's perception that criminals have certain personality characteristics that lead to some fifty-two errors in thinking. The modality teaches children to accept responsibility for their behaviors.

reality therapy   Modality encourages the three R's; realistic, responsibility and right-and-wrong. Assumes that meeting the basic needs of children will encourage responsible behavior.

secondary prevention   Prevention strategies aimed at trying to change the attitudes and behavior of a specific offender to become more compliant and law abiding.

teen courts   Community court model that utilizes nonjudical members to adjudicate minor offenses. Four types are, Adult Judge (most common), Youth Judge, Tribunal, and Peer Jury.

tertiary prevention   Prevention strategies aimed at reducing recidivism by discouraging the offender from repeating their offenses.

transactional analysis   Modality of therapy that is based on interpreting and evaluating personal relationships. Meaning is attached to "tape" of the past and offender ultimately will negotiate his or her own treatment.

youth service bureaus   Diversionary agencies that offered a variety of alternatives for youth to minimize youthful offending. Programs ranged from drop-in recreational centers to twenty-four hours crisis centers. Lack of funding closed many YSB's in the 1980's.

Practice Test

Multiple Choice

1. The vignette at the beginning of the chapter involved a crime committed by Karl, a 15 year old dropout. His crime was _____.
a. possession of marijuana
b. robbery
c. prostitution
d. stealing computers from the school
e. murder

2. One of the following is not one of the three different levels of delinquency prevention.
a. primary prevention
b. secondary prevention
c. tertiary prevention
d. permanent prevention

3. Intervention in the lives of juveniles or groups identified as being in circumstances that dispose them toward delinquency is called _____.
a. primary prevention
b. secondary prevention
c. tertiary prevention
d. permanent prevention

4. Programs that are directed at the prevention of recidivism are called _____.
a. primary prevention
b. secondary prevention
c. tertiary prevention
d. permanent prevention

5. Modifying conditions in the physical and social environment that lead to delinquency is called
_____.
a. primary prevention
b. secondary prevention
c. tertiary prevention
d. permanent prevention

6. Derrick Thomas was once a juvenile delinquent. He ended up being a _____.
a. inmate in Attica
b. murder victim in a bar fight
c. a linebacker for the Kansas City Chiefs
d. a police officer in Chicago
e. none of the above

7. A quick and generally inadequate remedy for complex problems is sometimes called a
_____. Typically they take a piecemeal approach to satisfy public perceptions about juvenile justice problems and solutions.
a. solution
b. panacea
c. problem solver
d. analysis

8. Lundman, McFarlane, and Scarpitti, when studying juvenile studies concluded _____
a. that most delinquency preventions programs are reducing delinquency
b. it appears unlikely that any of these projects prevented delinquent behavior
c. that different projects worked well with different types of delinquency
d. that delinquency was falling due to population changes not program design

9. The Chicago Area Project was initiated by _____ and his colleagues in the 1930s.
a. Edwin Sutherland
b. Albert Cohen
c. Robert Merton
d. Jennifer Rossi
e. Clifford Shaw

10. The Blueprints for Violence Prevention, was developed by The Center for the Study and Prevention of Violence at the _____.
a. University of Colorado—Boulder
b. University of Michigan
c. Michigan State University
d. University of California---Berkley
e. University of New York---Albany

11. The Big Brothers and Big Sisters of America Program is best know for being a (an) _____ program.
a. anti-drug
b. anti-gang
c. anti-drunk driving
d. mentoring
e. foster care

12. The public health model of dealing with juvenile crime focuses on _____.
a. psychological counseling
b. group home counseling
c. reducing risk and increasing resiliency
d. punishing the offender
e. getting the delinquent off of the street with some type of incarceration

13. The Model Programs Guide is designed to _____.
a. assist law enforcement in the apprehension of delinquents
b. assist counselors in guide group interaction with delinquents
c. assist practitioners and communities in implementing evidence-based prevention and intervention programs that can make a difference in the lives of children and communities.
d. assist educators in improving academic test scores for children

14. The _____ program aims to restructure the social environment of primary and secondary schools in order to provide fewer opportunities for bullying and to reduce the peer approval and support that reward bullying behavior.
a. Life Skills Training
b. Bully Prevention
c. Functional Family Therapy
d. Functional Family Therapy
e. Midwestern Prevention Project

15. The target population of this program is children aged two to eight who exhibit or are at risk for conduct problems.
a. Life Skills Training
b. Bully Prevention
c. Functional Family Therapy
d. Functional Family Therapy
e. Incredible Years: Parent, Teacher, and Child Training Series

16. This program is a three-year intervention curriculum designed to prevent or reduce use of "gateway" drugs such as tobacco, alcohol, and marijuana; the lessons emphasize social resistance skills training to help students identify pressures to use drugs.
a. Life Skills Training
b. Bully Prevention
c. Functional Family Therapy
d. Functional Family Therapy
e. Incredible Years: Parent, Teacher, and Child Training Series

17. Programs designed outside the formal juvenile justice system to provide alternatives for disposition of juvenile offenders are called _____.
a. juvenile institutions
b. halfway houses
c. day prison
d. diversion programs
e. parole

18. The most positive characteristic of traditional diversionary programs is that _____.
a. the public supports them
b. the police support them
c. they minimize the penetration of youthful offenders into the justice system
d. they apply equally to different types of offenders

19. There are four possible case-processing models that can be used by teen court. In this type of model the case is presented to a youth jury by a youth or adult. The youth jury then questions the defendant directly.
a. adult judge model
b. youth judge model
c. tribunal model
d. peer jury model
e. victim model

20. There are four possible case-processing models that can be used by teen court. In this type of model an adult serves as judge and rules on legal terminology and courtroom procedure. Youth serve as attorneys, jurors, clerks, bailiffs, and so forth.
a. adult judge model
b. youth judge model
c. tribunal model
d. peer jury model
e. victim model

21. There are four possible case-processing models that can be used by teen court. In this type of model youth attorneys present the case to a panel of three youth judges, who decide the appropriate disposition for the defendant.
a. adult judge model
b. youth judge model
c. tribunal model
d. peer jury model
e. victim model

22. There are four possible case-processing models that can be used by teen court. The most common type is _____.
a. adult judge model
b. youth judge model
c. tribunal model
d. peer jury model
e. victim model

23. What is the most frequent disposition in teen court cases?
a. limited jail time
b. limited prison time
c. lost of the juvenile's privilege to drive a car
d. community service
e. attachment of a juvenile's wages

24. Teen courts handle _____
a. only felony cases
b. usually only first time offenders
c. only drug cases
d. juveniles with a history of delinquency
e. all of the above

25. The purpose of a juvenile mediation program is _____.
a. bring all of the parties together so that the judge can determine the correct sentence
b. bring all of the parties together to resolve differences without court involvement
c. bring all of the parties together to determine who is guilty and who is not guilty
d. all of the above
e. none of the above

26. Robert Martinson is best associated with the statement _____.
a. "they're all crazy"
b. " all kids are good"
c. "give them a break"
d. "there are no bad kids, only bad parents"
e. "nothing works"

27. The statistical tool of _____ has been developed to enable reviewers to combine findings from different experiments.
a. Chi-Squared
b. bifurcated analysis
c. meta-analysis
d. survey research
e. computer analysis

28. On the mean streets from East L.A. to South-Central L.A., gang members are leaving the thug life and trying to make in a 60-person business called _____.
a. Ghetto Boys
b. Alternative Living
c. Homeboy Industries
d. Opportunities
e. The Hip-Hop Shoppe

29. A modality of therapy that is based on interpreting and evaluating personal relationships is called _____. Meaning is attached to the "tape" of the past and the offender ultimately will negotiate his or her own treatment.
a. guided group interaction
b. behavior modification
c. reality therapy
d. transactional analysis
e. positive peer culture

30. A modality of therapy that encourages the three R's; realistic, responsibility and right-and-wrong is called _____. It assumes that meeting the basic needs of children will encourage responsible behavior.
a. guided group interaction
b. behavior modification
c. reality therapy
d. transactional analysis
e. positive peer culture

True/False:

1. Primary prevention deals with the prevention of recidivism.

2. Secondary prevention is intervention in the lives of juveniles or groups identified as being in circumstances that dispose them toward delinquency.

3. A number of studies in the 1970s examined the effectiveness of delinquency prevention programs. Michael C. Dixon and William W. Wright concluded from their examination that many of these programs were working quite well in preventing delinquency.

4. The Big Brothers and Big Sisters of America operates the best known and largest mentoring program in the nation.

5. Research has shown that delinquency prevention programs focusing heavily on improving resiliency and ignoring the source of risk are very successful.

6. There are four possible case-processing models that can be used by teen court. In this type of model youth attorneys present the case to a panel of three youth judges, who decide the appropriate disposition for the defendant. It is called a Tribunal.

7. Teen courts handle a variety of offenders including drug cases, assault cases and juveniles with prior arrest records.

8. The purpose of a juvenile mediation program is to bring all involved parties together to resolve differences without court involvement.

9. Robert Martinson announced on *60 Minutes* that "there is evidence that many of the new juvenile counseling programs are working and reducing recidivism".

10. Positive reinforcement produces more effective and enduring behavior changes than negative punishment.

Fill-in-the-blank:

1. A psychological treatment method that rewards appropriate behavior positively, immediately, and systematically and assumes that rewards increase the occurrence of desired behavior is called _____.

2. Organized efforts to forestall or prevent the development of delinquent behaviors is called _____.

3. Dispositional alternatives for youthful offenders that exist outside of the formal juvenile justice system is known as _____.

4. Treatment modalities in which drug-abusing juveniles are usually treated in a group context is referred to as _____.

5. A counseling technique that involves treating all members of a family and a widely used method of dealing with a delinquent's socially unacceptable behavior is know as _____.

6. Interaction that places youthful offenders in an intensive group environment under the direction of an adult leader who substitutes a whole new structure of beliefs, values, and behaviors of the delinquent is called _____.

7. Special courts designed for nonviolent youthful offenders with substance abuse problems who require integrated sanctions and services such as mandatory drug testing, substance abuse treatment, supervised release, and aftercare are known as _____.

8. The claim made by Robert Martinson and his colleagues in the mid-1970s that correctional treatment is ineffective in reducing recidivism of correctional clients is know as

_____.

9. A group treatment modality that aims to build a positive youth subculture and encompasses a strategy that extends to all aspects of daily life is known as _____.

10. Efforts to reduce delinquency by modifying conditions in the physical and social environments that lead to juvenile crime is called _____.

11. A treatment method in which various adaptations of Freudian therapy are used by psychiatrists, clinical psychologists, and psychiatric social workers to encourage delinquents to talk about past conflicts that cause them to express emotional problems through aggressive or antisocial behavior is known as _____.

12. A cognitive restructuring strategy that seeks to identify delinquents' thinking errors (blaming others, trying to control or manipulate, failing to empathize, wanting to play the victim, etc) and then to help young offenders "own" and control their behaviors is called _____.

13. A treatment modality developed by William Glasser and G. L. Harrington and based on the principle that individuals must accept responsibility for their behavior is known as

_____.

14. Intervention in the lives of juveniles or groups who have been identified as being in circumstances that dispose them toward delinquency is called _____.

15. Voluntary nonjudicail forums, also known as youth courts, that keep minor offenders out of the formal justice system are called _____.

16. Programs directed at the prevention of recidivism among youthful offenders are called

_____.

17. A therapy, based on interpreting and evaluating personal relationships, that has proven to be of immediate value to many delinquents which uses several easy steps to make them feel "OK" is called _____.

Essay:

1. What are the three different levels of delinquency prevention?

2. The public health model employs a four step procedure to identify issues that need attention and to develop solutions. Explain each of these four steps.

3. Joy Dryfoos's 1990s analysis of the 100 most successful delinquency prevention programs tried through the 1980s identified seven common program components. Explain each of those seven components.

4. There are four possible case-processing models that can be used by teen court. Explain each of those four models.

5. Briefly explain transactional analysis.

6. Briefly explain reality therapy.

7. Briefly explain behavior modification.

8. Briefly explain guided group interaction.

9. Briefly explain positive peer culture.

Multiple Choice:
1. Answer: a   2. Answer: d   3. Answer: b   4. Answer: c   5. Answer: a   6. Answer: c
7. Answer: b   8. Answer: b   9. Answer: e   10. Answer: a   11. Answer: d   12. Answer: c
13. Answer: c   14. Answer: b   15. Answer: e   16. Answer: a   17. Answer: d
18. Answer: c   19. Answer: d   20. Answer: a   21. Answer: c   22. Answer: a
23. Answer: d   24. Answer: b   25. Answer: b   26. Answer: e   27. Answer: c
28. Answer: c   29. Answer: d   30. Answer: c

True/False:
1. False 2. True   3. False   4. True   5. False   6. True   7. False   8. True   9. False
10. True

Fill-in-the-blank:
1. behavior modification
2. delinquency prevention
3. diversion programs
4. drug and alcohol abuse interventions
5. family therapy
6. guided group interaction (GGI)
7. juvenile drug courts
8. "nothing works"
9. positive peer culture
10. primary prevention
11. psychotherapy
12. rational emotive therapy
13. reality therapy
14. secondary prevention
15. teen courts
16. tertiary prevention programs
17. transactional analysis

WEBSITES

Read the OJJDP publication, *Blueprints for Violence Prevention,* at www.justicestudies.com/weblibrary

Read the OJJDP publication, *YouthBuild U.S.A.,* at www.justicestudies.com/weblibrary

Read the OJJDP publication, *Juvenile Drug Court Programs,* at www.justicestudies.com/weblibrary

Visit AfterSchool.gov via www.justicestudies.com/webplaces

Visit the National Mentoring Partnership Web site via www.justicestudies.com/webplaces

Visit the National Youth Prevention Resource Center's Center's Web site via www.justicestudies.com/webplaces

Visit the National Center for Mental Health and Juvenile Justice Web's site via www.justicestudies.com/webplaces

Visit the National Youth Court Center's Web site via www.justicestudies.com/webplaces

www.grandviewyouthcourt.com/

www.brunswick.oh.us/police/index.htm

CHAPTER 13: THE JUVENILE JUSTICE PROCESS

LEARNING OBJECTIVES

After reading this chapter, you should be able to answer the following questions:

1. What is the juvenile justice process?

2. What are the stages in the juvenile justice process?

3. In what ways are the juvenile and adult justice systems the same?

4. Why is understanding the violent juvenile the key to effective interventions with juvenile offenders?

5. Why is minority over-representation such a serious issue for the juvenile justice system?

6. What will the juvenile justice system look like in the future?

CHAPTER SUMMARY

This chapter examines the organizational context of correcting and controlling juvenile delinquency, and crime in the United States. The *subsystems* of the juvenile justice system are the *police, juvenile courts*, and *corrections*. The functions of each subsystem vary in size and organization. However, most entities of juvenile justice are concerned with maintaining an equilibrium and survival. Most improvements in the juvenile justice system hardly seem to have scratched the surface in effectively dealing with the basic problem of youth crime in America.

Lack of cooperation and communication between the subsystems of juvenile justice, have helped to create a fragmented system of justice for youthful offenders. Lack of common goals, and local biases, help formulate a negative impact on juvenile offenders. The traditional correctional models may all seek a common goal to correct delinquent behavior, but they are not in agreement over what and when they should be used. The basic four discussed are, (1) the *Rehabilitation Model*, (2) the *Justice Model*, (3) the *Balanced and Restorative Model*, and (4) the *Crime Control Model*. The Crime Control Model is probably the most favored model and has wide support. Between 1992 and 1997, state legislatures in 47 states passed laws making the juvenile justice system more punitive. Recently, a trend toward a balanced approach is seen even more in the late 1990s.

The Juvenile Justice and Delinquency Prevention Act of 1974 required the *deinstitutionalization* of *status offenders* and the separation of juvenile delinquents from adult offenders. Amendments in 1980 and additionally, in 1992 required that juveniles be removed from adult jails and states must demonstrate efforts to reduce disparity in minority confinements. Today, jurisdictions still violate these requirements on the contention they have no alternatives available to them.

The return of *graduated sanctions* (indeterminate sentencing) is experiencing a new resurgence in adult corrections and the same movement is beginning to gain momentum in juvenile justice as well. Literature on correctional programs for juveniles, suggest that more effective interventions for at-risk-youth are warranted if certain key areas are addressed. Bartollas offers trend predictions for the future to help those understand which direction the system needs to move toward.

LECTURE OUTLINE

Introduction
- An Interview with Marty Beyer

I. Development of the Juvenile Justice System: The Origins of the Juvenile Court

A. Sociocultural Context
- Threes social conditions; (1) jailing children with adults, (2) Chicago's population tripled between 1880 and 1890 which brought filth, corruption, poverty and widespread disenchantment, and (3) higher status given to middle-class women led to child-saving avocation outside the home.

B. Legal Context
- Juvenile court founded in Cook County (Chicago) in 1899 based on the parens patriae doctrine.

C. Political Context
- The juvenile court satisfied the middle-class child-saving movement for offenders.

D. Economic Context
- Large scale immigration and class favoritism toward the middle classes.
- Child-savers were viewed as rescuing immigrant children to protect them from their families.

E. Emergence of Community Based Corrections.
- Expansion and Retrenchment in the Twentieth Century
- The development of Juvenile Institutions
- Twentieth-Century Changes

II. The Juvenile Justice System Today

A. Structures and Functions
- Justice system is comprised of *three subsystems, police, juvenile courts* and *corrections*.

- Equilibrium is a concern, changes in one causes consequences elsewhere.
- Police systems are oriented to law enforcement and order maintenance.
- Juvenile court is responsible for disposing of cases, parens patriae charges the court with treating rather than punishing youngsters.
- Corrections is responsible for care of the offenders. *Probation* is the most widely used disposition. Day treatment and residential programs are charged with preparing youths for their return to the community and humane care. Long term holding facilities are responsible for ensuring residents receive their constitutional rights.

B. Stages in the Juvenile Justice Process
- *Intake* process occurs in which a juvenile might remain in the community or be placed in detention or shelter facilities. More serious cases typically receive a petition, rather than informal adjustments.
- Transfer to adult court must occur prior to any juvenile proceedings or an *adjudicatory hearing* takes place to determine guilt or innocence.
- Disposition hearings occur after *adjudication* has found a juvenile delinquent. Most codes now require that disposition and adjudication occur at different times.
- Juveniles can be placed in public or privately administered day treatment or residential programs. Larger states with several facilities may use diagnostic centers to aid in determining proper institutional placement.
- *Aftercare* normally follows release from the institution.

C. Recidivism in the Juvenile Justice System
- Early cohort studies suggested that housing juveniles with adults increased the probability of juveniles becoming adult offenders.
- A recent Maricopa County cohort study contends that juvenile justice system contact by offenders reduced their propensity to recidivate (54 percent of males and 73 percent of females never returned). Recidivism is higher for males.

F. Comparison of the Juvenile and Adult Justice Systems
- Both systems are made up of three subsystems.
- Vocabulary is different for juvenile systems, yet the intent is the same.
- Both systems are under fire to get *tough* on crime. Most deal with overloads, and overcrowding, face funding problems and burnout.

III. Basic Correctional Models

A. Four basic correctional models: (1) *Rehabilitative*, (2) *Justice*, (3) *Balanced and Restorative Justice* and (4) *Crime Control*.

- The rehabilitative modality seeks to change an offender's character, attitude, or behavior patterns. The *medical, adjustment*, and *reintegration* models are all expressions of the rehabilitative philosophy.
- The medical model contends delinquency is caused by factors that can be cured and punishment should be avoided as it only reinforces negative self-image.

- The adjustment model purports that delinquents need treatment that will demonstrate responsible behavior.
- The basic assumption of the reintegration model is that delinquent's problems must be solved in the community where the problems originated
- The justice model (just deserts) holds that punishment is the basic purpose of juvenile justice.
- The balanced and restorative model is an integrated model and seeks to reconcile the interests of victims, offenders, and the community through supervision programs.
- The crime control model is based on classical school criminology, which emphasizes punishment and that life and property of the innocent should be protected.

B. Emerging Approach to Handling Youthful Offenders
- The crime control model has the largest support for serious and violent offenders. States between 1992 and 1997 enacted laws to make the juvenile system more punitive.
- The trend in the late 1990s was a movement toward a balanced approach.

IV. The Juvenile Justice and Delinquency Prevention Act of 1974
- The Act recommends that status offenses be handled outside the court system and there be separation of juvenile and adult offenders.
- In 1980 an amendment to the Act required that juveniles be removed from adult jails and lockup facilities.
- In 1992 another amendment to the 1974 Act required that states determine the extent of disproportionate confinement of minorities and reduce the disparities.

A. Race and Juvenile Justice

B. Deinstitutionalization of Status Offenders
- More attempts are made to separate status offenders from delinquents.

C. Removal of Juveniles for Jails and Lockups
- Several states have enacted legislation prohibiting the jailing of juveniles with adults.

D. Disproportionate Minority Confinement
- Mounting evidence of unfair evidence of minority confinement.

V. Graduated Sanctions
- Increased attention given to indeterminate sanctions to reduce delinquency.

A. Core Principles of Graduated Sanctions
- A model system combines the treatment and rehabilitation of youth with fair, humane, reasonable, and appropriate sanctions.
- General characteristics include, key areas of risk in a youth's life, strengthen the personal and institutional factors contributing to healthy adolescent development.

VI. Trends for the Future

- It is like that the adult system will become more involved with older offenders.
- There is concerned that with a projected increased juvenile population the juvenile justice system will have greater demands on it.
- Many of these juveniles will come from impoverished homes headed by single mothers, and concern exists that this may mean more minorities in the juvenile justice system.
- With the increase population of poor juveniles the rate of juvenile violence, including homicides may again grow.
- The widespread feeling among many in the American population today is that there are more troubled teenagers than in the past.
- The field of adolescent psychiatry will be more frequently called upon to treat troubled youths.
- Some argue that stiffer penalties could be a deterrent to juveniles who might otherwise kill.
- Gangs are perceived as a serious social problem, but there is a lack of agreement about what to do to reduce the treat of gang violence.
- The use of drugs by adolescents remains an issue in American society.
- Many adolescents consume alcohol to excess.
- Debate has focused for some time on the disparity of juvenile court sentencing.
- State legislatures are increasingly passing laws intended to deter juvenile crime.

KEY TERMS

adjudicatory hearing   The juvenile trial stage in which evidence is presented to reach a finding as to the level of guilt or innocence of a juvenile offender.

adjustment model   A model of juvenile rehabilitation that focuses on teaching offenders to be accountable for their actions.

aftercare   Supervision of juveniles that is designed to make an optimal resocialization and adjustment back into community living, after they have been released from correctional institutions.

balanced and restorative model   An integrative correctional model that seeks to reconcile the interests of victims, offenders, and the community through programs and supervision ractices.

child savers   The name given to an organized group of progressive social reformers of the late nineteenth and early twentieth centuries who promoted numerous laws aimed at protecting children and institutionalizing an idealized image of childhood innocence.

commitment   The sentence of confinement given to a juvenile offender at the disposition stage of the juvenile court proceedings.

cottage system A widely used treatment practice that places small groups of training school residents into cottages. (shall housing units)

detention The holding of a juvenile offender in jail.

dispositional hearing The sentencing stage of a juvenile proceeding in which the judge decides what an appropriate sanction should be given for a particular offense(s).

disproportionate minority confinement The court-ordered confinement, in juvenile institutions, of members of minority groups in numbers disproportionate to their representation in the general population

intake The first stage of the juvenile justice process in which the decision is made to divert the offender or file a juvenile court petition. Typically completed by juvenile probation or police officers.

juvenile court officer A person who typically processes juveniles entering the juvenile court system.

justice model A model of juvenile justice that holds that punishment is pivotal in deterring delinquency and that violators deserved to be punished.

medical model A model of rehabilitation that suggests that delinquency is caused by factors that can be identified, isolated, treated and cured.

petition The indictment document filed into juvenile court alleging the offense(s) committed by a juvenile offender.

probation officer Juvenile officer who supervises offenders assigned to their case list. Typically include formation of social histories, case files, and related enforcement duties of probation conditions.

reintegration model Community-based model of rehabilitation that focuses on restoring the offender back into the community and addresses the social responsibility of both the offender and community.

rehabilitative philosophy The basic tenets of the medical model, the adjustment model and the reintegration model which seeks to change an offender's character, attitude, or behavior.

residential programs Programs conducted for the rehabilitation of youth within community-based and institutional settings.

taking into custody The arrest process of physically taking a juvenile offender into custody.

training school A correctional facility for long-term placement of juvenile delinquents; may be public (ran by a state department of corrections or youth commission) or private.

Practice Test

Multiple Choice:

1. The vignette at the beginning of the chapter involved Lionel Tate, who was famous for being
_____.
a. a gang leader in Miami, Florida
b. an abandoned and abuse child found living under an interstate
c. murdered at his grade school
d. the youngest drug dealer in Miami
e. the youngest child in modern times to be sentenced to life imprisonment

2. How old was Lionel Tate?
a.   6
b.   8
c. 10
d. 12
e. 17

3. The juvenile justice system is made up of three subsystems. One of the following in not one
of those systems.
a. legislature
b. police
c. juvenile court
d. corrections

4. The juvenile court was founded in _____.
a. New York City
b. Chicago, Cook County
c. Pittsburg
d. Boston
e. Philadelphia

5. The juvenile court was founded in what year?
a. 1866
b. 1899
c. 1917
d. 1939
e. 1951

6. A medieval English doctrine that sanctioned the right of the Crown to intervene as parent for the child's welfare was called _____.
a. the Power of the King
b. the Child Savers
c. parens patriae
d. in loco parentis

7. In *The Child Savers* it is argued that the juvenile court was an extension of _____.
a. lower class values
b. liberal values
c. middle class values
d. the values of the rich

8. Zebulon Brockway was the first superintendent of _____.
a. The Boston Home for Boys
b. The New York City Boys Club
c. The Child Savings Institution in Chicago
d. The Elmira Reformatory in New York
e. None of the above

9. John Augustus is know as _____.
a. the "Father of Parole"
b. the "Father of the Juvenile Court"
c. the "Father of Juvenile Institutions"
d the "Father of Probation"
e. all of the above

10. The concept of probation was started in _____.
a. New York
b. Chicago
c. Boston
d. Philadelphia
e. Pittsburg

11. The New Jersey Experimental Project for the treatment of Youthful Offenders was also know as _____.
a. Elmira Reformatory
b. The Highfields Project
c. The New Jersey Project
d. the Residential Treatment Center
e. The Reagan Center (It was funded by the Reagan Administration)

12. The first House of Refuge in America was _____.
a. The Boston Children's Home
b. The Franklin Home in Philadelphia
c. The Chicago House of Refuge
d. The New York House of Refuge
e. The Philadelphia Boy Home

13. Before the end of the eighteenth century, the _____ was commonly believed to be the source or cause of deviance.
a. devil
b. school system
c. economy
d. race of a person
e. family

14. A system of housing developed in 1854 to house smaller groups of youths in separate buildings, usually no more than twenty to forty youths per unit is called the _____.
a. college system
b. family structure system
c. cottage system
d. open dorm system
e. none of the above

15. The intake officer is usually a _____.
a. police officer
b. prosecuting attorney
c. the judge
d. the parole officer
e. the probation officer

16. Lee Boyd Malvo was know for _____.
a. being a juvenile serial rapists
b. being the juvenile at Columbine who shot 13 other students
c. being one of the Beltway Killers
d. starting the Vice Lords
e. starting the Gangster Disciples

17. The prosecutor in juvenile court language is called a _____.
a. district attorney
b. solicitor
c. juvenile prosecutor
d. commonwealth attorney
e. petitioner

18. The sentencing hearing in juvenile court language is called a _____.
a. dispositional hearing
b. decision hearing
c. outcome disposition
d. verdict
e. sentencing hearing

19. An indictment in juvenile court language is called _____.
a. a warrant
b. a charge
c. a petition
d. an information
e. an accusation

20. A defense attorney in juvenile court language is called _____.
a. a solicitor
b. the defender
c. the helper
d. the assister
e. a respondent

21. To change the offender's character, attitudes, or behavior patterns in order to diminish his or her propensities for youth crime is characteristic of the _____.
a. crime control model
b. balance or restorative model
c. rehabilitation model
d. justice model
e. the punishment model

22. The _____ holds to the belief that punishment should be the basic purpose of the juvenile justice system.
a. crime control model
b. balance or restorative model
c. rehabilitation model
d. justice model
e. the education model

23. An integrated model that seeks to reconcile the interests of victims, offenders, and the community through programs and supervision practices is called the _____. This model seeks to ensure accountability to crime victims and to enhance community safety.
a. crime control model
b. balance or restorative model
c. rehabilitation model
d. justice model
e. the education model

24. The _____ is grounded on its adherents' conviction that the first priority of justice should be the protection of the life and property of the innocent.
a. crime control model
b. balance or restorative model
c. rehabilitation model
d. justice model
e. the education model

25. This model of juvenile justice is more concerned that the juvenile delinquent receives therapy.
a. crime control model
b. balance or restorative model
c. rehabilitation model
d. justice model
e. the education model

26. Which of the following four models of juvenile justice does not have as its base the concept of free will?
a. crime control model
b. balance or restorative model
c. rehabilitation model
d. justice model
e. the education model

27. Which of the following four models of juvenile justice has the indeterminate sentence as part of its philosophy?
a. crime control model
b. balance or restorative model
c. rehabilitation model
d. justice model
e. the education model

28. Which of the following four models of juvenile justice views treatment as ineffective and a method of coddling offenders?
a. crime control model
b. balance or restorative model
c. rehabilitation model
d. justice model
e. the education model

29. Which of the following four models of juvenile justice views the purpose as sentencing as doing justice.
a. crime control model
b. balance or restorative model
c. rehabilitation model
d. justice model
e. the education model

30. Anthony Platt is author of the famous book, _____.
a. *David Copperfield*
b. *Hackberry Finn*
c. *The Child Savers*
d. *The Last Child*
e. *There are no Children Here*

True/False:

1. Research on juveniles has demonstrated that stricter punishments by the juvenile justice system are likely to eliminate recidivism.

2. For his crimes, Lee Boyd Malvo received a sentence of capital punishment.

3. According to the authors, there is wide support for using the crime control model with the serious and violent juvenile.

4. The Justice Model of juvenile justice believes in the concept of free will.

5. The Justice Model of juvenile justice believes in the indeterminate sentence.

6. Juveniles are allowed to be house in adult jails as long as they are not in the same cell.

7. Rates of homicides are higher for minorities then they are for white youthful offenders.

8. White juvenile delinquents appear to be disproportionately involved in robbery, aggravated assault and rape.

9. There is concern that with a projected increased juvenile population in the next twenty years greater demands will be made on the juvenile justice system.

10. The authors argue that the use of restorative justice has hit its peak and will decline in the next decade.

Fill-in-the-blank:

1. The stage of juvenile court proceedings that usually includes the child's plea, presentation of evidence by the prosecution and defense, cross-examination of witnesses, and a finding by the judge as to whether the allegations in the petition can be sustained is known as a _____.

2. A rehabilitative correctional approach that emphasizes helping delinquents demonstrate responsible behavior is a(n) _____.

3. The supervision of juveniles who are released from correctional institutions so they can make an optimal adjustment to community living; or the status of a juvenile conditionally released from a treatment or confinement facility and placed under supervision in the community is called _____.

4. An integrative correctional model that seeks to reconcile the interests of victims, offenders, and the community through programs and supervised practices is known as a _____.

5. A name given to an organized group of progressive social reformers of the late nineteenth and early twentieth centuries who promoted numerous laws aimed at protecting children and institutionalizing an idealized image of childhood innocence is called _____.

6. A determination made by a juvenile judge at the disposition stage of a juvenile court proceeding that a juvenile is to be sent to a juvenile correctional institution is called a _____.

7. A correctional model supported by James Q. Wilson, Ernest van den Haag, and others, who believe that discipline and punishment are the most effective means of deterring youth crime is know as the _____.

8. The temporary restraint of a juvenile in a secure facility, usually because he or she is acknowledged to be dangerous either to self or others is called _____.

9. The stage of the juvenile court proceedings in which the juvenile judge decides the most appropriate placement for a juvenile who has been adjudicated a delinquent, a status offender, or a dependent child is called a _____.

10. A philosophical underpinning of the justice model which holds that juveniles deserve to be punished if they violated the law, and the punishment must be proportionate to the seriousness of the offense is known as _____.

11. David Fogel's justice model, which advocates that it is necessary to be fair, reasonable, humane, and constitutional in the implementation of justice is called _____.

12. A justice systems model based on the belief that individuals have free will and are responsible for their decisions and thus deserve to be punished if they violate the law, and the punishment they receive should be proportionate to the offense is called the _____.

13. A probation officer who serves juveniles is a _____.

14. A correctional model whose proponents believe that delinquency is cause by factors that can be identified, isolated, treated, and cured – much like a disease is known as the _____.

15. A person who is under the age of legal consent is called a _____.

16. A document, or _____, filed in juvenile court alleging that a juvenile is a delinquent and asking that the court assume jurisdiction over the juvenile; or asking an alleged delinquent be waived to criminal court for prosecution as an adult.

17. In the juvenile justice system, an intake officer (prosecutor) who seeks court jurisdiction over a youthful offender is referred to as a _____.

18. The repetition of delinquent behavior by a youth who has been released from probation status or from training school is called _____.

19. A correctional model whose goal is to change an offender's character, attitudes, or behavior so as to diminish his or her delinquent propensities is a _____.

20. A perspective that holds the offenders' problems must be solved in the community in which they occur and that community-based organizations can help them readjust to community life is called a _____.

21. The defense attorney in the juvenile court system is called a _____.

22. The process of arresting a juvenile for socially unacceptable or unlawful behavior is known as _____.

23. Programs conducted for the rehabilitation of youth within community-based and institutional settings are known as _____.

24. A correctional facility for long-term placement of juvenile delinquents; which may be public or private is called a _____.

25. A widely used treatment practice that places small groups of training school residents into cottages is called a _____.

26. The court-ordered confinement, in juvenile institutions, of members of minority groups in numbers disproportionate to their representation in the general population is known as _____.

Essay:

1. Using Anthony Platt's *The Childs Savers* describe Platt's position o the origins and purposes of the juvenile court.

2. To correct the behavior of the juvenile delinquent, there have traditionally been four basic correctional models. Explain in detail each of those four models.

3. What evidence does Janet Lauritsen present to support the differential offending hypothesis.

4. The text lists fifteen trends facing the juvenile justice system. Describe at least ten of those fifteen trends.

5. Explain the rehabilitative model of juvenile justice with its three subsystem.

6. Explain the justice model of juvenile justice.

7. explain the crime control model of juvenile justice.

8. Explain the balanced and restorative model of juvenile justice.

Answers Practice Test

Multiple Choice:
1. Answer: e   2. Answer: d   3. Answer: a   4. Answer: b   5. Answer: b   6. Answer: c
7. Answer: c   8. Answer: d   9. Answer: d   10. Answer: c   11. Answer: b   12. Answer: d
13. Answer: e   14. Answer: c   15. Answer: e   16. Answer: c   17. Answer: e
18. Answer: a   19. Answer: c   20. Answer: e   21. Answer: c   22. Answer: d
23. Answer: b   24. Answer: a   25. Answer: c   26. Answer: c   27. Answer: c
28. Answer: a   29. Answer: d   30. Answer: c

True/False:
1. False 2. False   3. True   4. True   5. False   6. False   7. True   8. False   9. True
10. False

Fill-in-the-blank:
1. adjudicatory hearing
2. adjustment model
3. aftercare
4. balanced and restorative model
5. child saves
6. commitment
7. crime control model
8. detention
9. dispositional hearing
10. just deserts
11. justice as fairness
12. justice model
13. juvenile court officer
14. medical model
15. minor
16. petition
17. petitioner
18. recidivism
19. rehabilitation model
20. reintegration model
21. respondent
22. taking into custody
23. residential programs
24. training school
25 cottage system
26. disproportionate minority confinement

WEBSITES

Read Chapter 4 of the OJJDP publication, *Juvenile Offenders and Victims: 2006 National Report,* at www.justicestudies.com/weblibrary

Read the OJJDP publication, *How the Justice System Responds to Juvenile Victims: A Comprehensive Model*, at www.justicestudies.com/weblibrary

Read the OJJDP publication, *Juveniles Facing Criminal Sanctions: Three States That Changed the Rules,* at www.justicestudies.com/weblibrary

Read the OJJDP Juvenile Justice Bulletin, *Restorative Justice Conferences as an early Response to Young Offenders,* at www.justicestudies.com/weblibrary

Read the NIJ article, *Brick by Brick: Dismantling the Border Between Juvenile and Adult Justice,* at www.justicestudies.com/weblibrary

Learn more about Disproportionate Minority Contact (DMC) from the Juvenile Justice Evaluation Center Online via www.justicestudies.com/webplaces

Visit the American Bar Association's Juvenile Justice Committee online via www.justicestudies.com/webplaces

Visit the Coalition for Juvenile Justice's Web site via www.justicestudies.com/webplaces

View the OJJDP PowerPoint presentation "Juvenile Justice System Structure and Process", at www.justicestudies.com/webplaces

www.ncjrs.org/txtfiles/ojjjjact.txt

www.criminology.fsu.edu/jjclearinghouse/jj19.html

CHAPTER 14: THE POLICE AND THE JUVENILE

LEARNING OBJECTIVES

After reading this chapter you should be able to answer the following questions:

1. What has been the history of police-juvenile relations?

2. How have the attitudes of juveniles changed toward the police?

3. How are juvenile offenders processed?

4. What are the legal rights of juveniles in encounters with police?

5. What kinds of efforts do police make to deter delinquency?

6. How does community police impact juveniles?

CHAPTER SUMMARY

In the late 1800s and early 1900s, the policing of juveniles was viewed differently from the policing of adults. The progressive movement encouraged many social reforms and policing was affected as well. The main focus was on prevention of juvenile delinquency and the development of specialized units to work with juveniles. By the late 1970s and early 1980s, police involvement tended to decline in delinquency prevention and police diversionary programs. Budgetary constraints and specialization encouraged police departments to move away from intensive involvement in juvenile relations. However, by the late 1980s and early 1990s, police once again were encouraged to refocus their efforts on prevention. The latest emphasis of police intervention has been attributed to the rise of juvenile violence and proliferation of youth gangs.

The importance of police-juvenile relations cannot be minimized because the police are generally the first contact juveniles have with the justice system. Today, juveniles have better attitudes toward police than in the past. Police have wide *discretion* in regard to juvenile law violations. Studies reveal that police divert 80 percent to 90 percent of juvenile encounters away from the juvenile justice system. The seriousness of the offense is the key element influencing police-juvenile discretion.

Juveniles have won due process rights in several legal procedural areas. In *State v. Lowry* (1967), the Fourth Amendment protection against unreasonable searches was granted to juveniles. The application of *Miranda rights* has affected police excesses in regard to *police interrogations* of juveniles. The *Gault* case (1967) was instrumental in awarding juveniles most due process rights, with the exclusion of jury trials, which is still applied on a state-by-state basis.

Police have concentrated recent efforts on reduction of violent youth crime. Their role in reducing juvenile availability to handguns is credited in playing a major role in reducing juvenile homicides in urban settings. Police continue to combat drug and gang problems along with the recent frustrations of hate crimes.

LECTURE OUTLINE

Introduction
- Murder in Miami

I. The History of Police-Juvenile Relations
- Seventeenth and eighteenth centuries use informal methods of control by family, church and community (mutual pledge and watch/ward systems).
- Organized police were largely uneducated, poorly paid and ill-treated (political corruption).
- NY police department began a program in 1914 to prevent juvenile delinquency, by 1924, 90 percent of the nation's cities had established juvenile programs (PAL in 1920).
- August Vollmer introduced the concept of *youth bureau* in 1930 at Berkeley, CA.

A. Contemporary Developments in Juvenile-Police Relations
- The role of juvenile officer developed after WW II with the Central States Juvenile Officers Association (1955) and International Juvenile Officers Association (1957) developing standards (the goal is to be helpful and not punitive).
- In the 1960s police became involved in truancy and drug prevention programs and actual supervision of youthful offenders.
- By the 1970s and 1980s the trend was for police to move away from deep involvement in juvenile work. Detective divisions assumed responsibilities in many departments.
- The 1990s proliferation of substance abuse resulted in police moving back into schools and providing security for gun-free zones and various other programs.

II. Juvenile's Attitudes Toward the Police
- Most attention to attitudes given in the 1970s.
- Whites have a more favorable opinion of police than African-Americans. Females have a more favorable opinion of police than males. Students from middle-and upper-class families have a better attitude toward police than lower class students.
- Juveniles with no police contact have more favorable views than juveniles with police contact.
- Sociocultural context shapes youth attitude toward police. Most youths today have a positive attitude toward police.

III. The Processing of Juvenile Offenders
- Influence of individual factors, sociocultural factors, and organizational factors affecting the processing of juvenile offenders.

A. Factors That Influence Police Discretion
- Police discretion if not used would increase the number of youths two to three times and make the system unmanageable.
- Nature of the offense (seriousness) is the most important factor.
- The number complaints and the presence of a citizen.
- Gender of the offender, girls are less likely to be referred than boys.
- Race of the offender, police are more likely to arrest minority juveniles.
- Socioeconomic status, more "saving" is performed with middle-and upper-class juveniles.
- Individual factors of prior arrest, age, peers and family situation and conduct.
- Nature of police-juvenile interaction and departmental policy.
- Media pressures and the socioeconomic status of the victim creating external pressure.

B. Informal and Formal Dispositions
- Warning and releasing youth back into the community (25 percent of cases in 1997).
- Station adjustment (official contact recorded)
- Referring to a diversion agency (1 percent in 1997)
- Issuing a citation and referral to court. In 1997, two-thirds of juvenile arrests were referred to court by intake officers.
- Detention centers where an intake worker can release offenders or leave them in detention if they pose a danger to themselves or others.

C. Police Attitudes toward Youth Crime
- Leniency of juvenile cases makes police feel the system is too permissive.
- Police know juveniles can be unpredictable and dangerous.
- Juveniles challenge police authority and police are reluctant to engage in encounters.

IV. The Legal Rights of Juveniles

A. Search and Seizure
- Search and seizure rights affirmed for juveniles with the State v. Lowry (1967) case.

B. Interrogation Practices
- Haley v. Ohio is an early case involving excesses in police interrogation of juveniles.
- Miranda v. Arizona (1967) entitles individuals to remain silent during interrogations, and the *In re Gault* case applied due process principles and right to counsel.
- Fare v. Michael C. (1979) decision applied the *totality of circumstances* to juveniles.
- Waiving of Miranda rights is regulated through state-by-state requirements.

C. Fingerprinting
- Some juvenile courts require that judicial approval is required to fingerprint juveniles.

- Police policy dictates the fingerprinting practice in some jurisdictions.

D. Pretrial Identification Practices
- The Juvenile Justice and Delinquency Prevention Act of 1974 recommended that photographs, lineups and media releases be prohibited.
- By 1997 45 states permitted photographing of juveniles for record purposes and 42 states allowed restricted media releases of juvenile crimes.

V. Prevention and Deterrence of Delinquency
- Community-based, school-based, and gang-based interventions are all part of police strategies used to prevent and deter youth crime.
- Community policing moves police from reactive policing to proactive policing, increases police accountability, and encourages police to view citizens as partners.

A. Community-Based Interventions
- Focuses on relations with school, community agencies, youth organizations, and youths themselves. (Curfew arrests increased dramatically to keep youths off the street).
- Drug arrests increased and efforts to get guns out of juvenile hands.
- AMBER Alert

B. School-Based Interventions
- Officer Friendly and McGruff programs were developed to improve relations between police and younger children.
- Gang Resistance Education and Training (GREAT) and Law-Related Education (LRE).
- LRE is designed to teach principles and skills to become responsible citizens. One study suggested juveniles were less likely to associate with delinquent peers after LRE training.
- DARE has been criticized for being ineffective in the long term.
- Officers (SROs) employed full-time in schools for a variety of preventative measures.

C. Gang-Based Interventions
- Three intervention strategies; youth service bureaus, gang details, and gang units.
- 85 percent of specialized gang units have been established since 1990.

KEY TERMS

arrest   The process of taking a juvenile into custody for an alleged violation of the law.

citation   Legal notification issued by police for a person(s) to appear in court to answer to a specific charge(s)

gang unit   A specialized unit found in some police agencies that is responsible for the prevention and intervention of gangs to reduce related crime.

juvenile officer Specialized assignment found in many police department and juvenile agencies for the sole prevention and reduction of juvenile related crime.

Miranda v. Arizona Landmark case that allows citizens to exercise their Fifth Amendment protection against self-incrimination by remaining silent when interrogated by law enforcement officers. The Gault (1967) case reaffirmed the application of the Miranda case to juveniles.

New Jersey v. T.L.O. 1985 Supreme Court ruling which allows police and school authorities to search student lockers and property without a search warrant based upon reasonableness of the search.

police discretion The use of personal judgment by a representative of the justice system during arrest, processing, or sentencing phases of the justice process.

police interrogation Process of questioning a person suspected to be involved in a criminal matter. Some states require juveniles to have parents or legal guardians present and do not allow juveniles to voluntarily waive their Miranda protection.

pretrial identification practices Process and practices include fingerprinting, photographing, and appearing in lineups. Some states require judicial approval for any pretrial process to occur. Recently, more states are allowing such practices without court approval.

search and seizure The Constitution requires police to obtain a lawful search warrant to search a person or property under their control. However, recent efforts to control drug and gang related crimes have led to Supreme Court rulings that have relaxed the requirements of warrant and warrantless searches.

station adjustment Disposition option whereby a juvenile is taken to the police station and then released after an official reprimand and contact is recorded.

Practice Test

Multiple Choice:

1. The vignette at the beginning of the chapter is about _____.
a. drug smuggling in Miami
b. the Latin Kings in New York
c. 18 young African-Americans being shot
d. police corruption and juveniles
e. police abuse of juveniles

2. In the 1870 the police were _____.
a. drawn from the least educated segment of society
b. were ill treated
c. were poorly paid
d. all of the above

3. The concept of a Youth Bureau was first introduced by _____.
a. Teddy Roosevelt
b. Jane Adams
c. August Vollmer
d. James A. Garfield
e. Zebulon Brockway

4. The first Youth Bureau in policing was in _____.
a. New York City
b. Chicago
c. Philadelphia
d. Boston
e. Berkeley

5. The Police Athletic League (PAL) is said to have started with a bang. What is meant by that in this context?
a. a juvenile had blown up a building
b. a juvenile had shot out a store window
c. a juvenile had thrown a rock through a window
d. a juvenile had out nails in the road causing a police car to have a blowout

6. Who began the Police Athletic League (PAL)?
a. Captain John Sweeney
b. Teddy Roosevelt
c. August Vollmer
d. Scott Decker
e. Zebulon Brockway

7. According to Scott Decker, who has the most negative attitudes toward the police?
a. older white men
b. older black men
c. younger white men
d. younger black men
e. older white women

8. The most important factor determining the disposition of the misbehaving juvenile is
_____.
a. his or her race
b. his or her educational level
c. the seriousness of the offense
d. the attitude of the officer
e. the time of day the stop was made

9. When the police stop a vehicle because of the race of the occupants it is called _____.
a. directed patrolling
b. problem oriented policing
c. community policing
d. police community relations
e. racial profiling

10. A legal notification issued by the police for a person to appear in court to answer to a specific charge is called a _____.
a. notice of intent
b. citation
c. notification
d. charge
e. indictment

11. In Canada, the juvenile has _____.
a. the right to remain silent
b. the right to have defense counsel
c. the right to contact counsel f other adults before questioning
d. all of the above
e. none of the about, these right only exist in America

12. Which Amendment protects Americans from unreasonable search and seizure?
a. first
b. fourth
c. fifth
d. sixth
e. eighth

13. In 1961, the case of _____ affirmed rights against unreasonable search and seizure for adults in state cases.
a. *Mapp v. Ohio*
b *In re Gault*
c. *Gideon v. Wainwright*
d. *Miranda v. Arizona*
e. *Haley v. Ohio*

14. The Supreme Court applied the ban against unreasonable search and seizure to juveniles in _____.
a. *Mapp v. Ohio*
b *State v. Lowry*
c. *Gideon v. Wainwright*
d. *Miranda v. Arizona*
e. *Haley v. Ohio*

15. The case of *Haley v. Ohio* dealt with the issue of _____.
a. a search of a car
b. a search of an apartment
c. a search of his dorm room
d. a search of his cooler containing beer
e. none of the above

16. Which case gave adults the right to remain silent, the right to have an attorney present during questioning, and the right to be assigned an attorney?
a. *Mapp v. Ohio*
b *Miranda v. Arizona*
c. *Gideon v. Wainwright*
d. *In re Gault*
e. *Haley v. Ohio*

17. Which case gave juveniles the right to remain silent, the right to have an attorney present during questioning, and the right to be assigned an attorney?
a. *Mapp v. Ohio*
b *Miranda v. Arizona*
c. *Gideon v. Wainwright*
d. *In re Gault*
e. *Haley v. Ohio*

18. Which case applied the "totality of the circumstances" principle to juvenile interrogations?
a. *Fare v. Michael C.*
b *Miranda v. Arizona*
c. *Gideon v. Wainwright*
d. *Miranda v. Arizona*
e. *Haley v. Ohio*

19. The rate that juveniles repeat sex crimes is about _____ .
a.   5-15%
b.   15-25%
c.   30-40%
d.   40-50%
e.   over 50 %

20. The 1994 crime bill provided 9 billion dollars for _____ .
a. research on terrorism
b. police community relations
c. problem oriented policing
d. community-oriented policing
e. SWAT teams

21. In an interview with Loren Evenrud he stated that the most obvious change in the police dealing with juveniles is _____ .
a. most juvenile are from other countries
b. most juveniles are unemployed
c. the increase in violence among the juvenile population
d. the increase in female offenders
e. he said all of these things

22. The national program to find missing children is called _____ .
a. D.A.R.E.
b. N.G.C.R.C.
c. G.R.A.C.E.
d. The Center for Missing Children
e. AMBER Alert

23. What percentage of homicides involving juveniles, (age 12 or older) are committed with a firearm?
a. 10%
b. 25%
c. 40%
d. 50%
e. 75%

24. What crime prevention program has as its motto, "Take a Bite Out of Crime"?
a. D.A.R.E.
b. N.G.C.R.C.
c. G.R.A.C.E.
d. The Center for Missing Children
e. McGruff, The Crime Dog

25. The D.A.R.E. program is designed to _____.
a. reduce the use of drugs
b. reduce the participation in gangs
c. reduce the amount of guns in our society
d. help find missing children
e. none of the above

26. The D.A.R.E. programs was developed in _____.
a. New York City
b. Boston
c. Chicago
d. Los Angeles
e. San Francisco

True/False:

1. Several studies have reported that juveniles who have contact with the police have more positive attitudes toward police than do those who have not had contact.

2. According to Winfree and Griffiths negative contacts with the police influence juvenile attitudes toward the police more than do the factors of sex, race, residence, or socioeconomic status.

3. Murty and colleagues found that younger African American males did not have hostile attitudes toward the police.

4. The more deeply committed a juvenile is to crime, the more hostile he or she is toward the police.

5. The most important factor determining the disposition of the misbehaving juvenile is race of the suspect.

6. A number of studies have found that the presence of a citizen or the complaint of a citizen is an important determining factor in the disposition of an incident involving a juvenile.

7. Traditionally, girls have been less likely than boys to be arrested and referred to the juvenile court for criminal offenses.

8. The police overall have more positive attitudes toward youthful offenders today than in the past.

9. The police, in large cities especially, think that youth crime is out of control because of the permissiveness of the juvenile court system.

10. Police-juvenile relations in Canada and Australia are totality different from police-juvenile relations in the United States.

11. Chinese police officers usually devote 90% of their time and resources to serving the community's various social and human needs.

12. To search a juvenile or to search a juvenile's room it in not required that the officer has a valid search warrant or probable cause.

13. The Fourth Amendment's guarantee against unreasonable searches and seizures does not apply to juveniles.

14. Because juvenile records are sealed and not public information, it is impossible for juveniles sex offenders to be listed on sex offender registries.

15. According to Mark Chaffin, if treated, juvenile sex offenders are far less likely to commit another sex offense.

16. The AMBER Alert system stand for Amber Hagerman who was kidnapped and brutally murdered while riding her bicycle.

Fill-in-the-blank:

1. The process of taking a person into custody for an alleged violation of the law is called
_____.

2. A summons to appear in juvenile court is a _____.

3. A pretrial identification procedure used with both juveniles and adults following arrest:
_____.

4. A specialized unit established by some police departments to address the problem of gangs is called a _____.

5. A police officer who has received specialized training to work effectively with juveniles in known as a _____.

6. The U.S. Supreme Court ruled that before any questioning can take place, suspects taken into custody must be informed they have the right to remain silent, anything they say may be used against them, and they have the right to legal counsel, is the famous 1966 case
_____.

7. A police officers ability to choose from among a number of alternative dispositions when handling a situation is known as _____.

8. Procedures such as fingerprinting, photographing, and placing juveniles in lineups for the purpose of identification prior to formal court appearance is known as _____.

9. The constitution requires a warrant for the authorized gathering of evidence by the police. This safeguard protects individuals against unlawful _____.

10. A disposition option available to a police officer whereby a juvenile is taken to the police station following a complaint, recorded, given an official reprimand, and then released to his or her parents or guardians is known as a(n) _____.

Essay:

1. What are the nine factors that can influence police discretion?

2. A patrol officer or juvenile officer has at least five options when investigating a complaint against a juvenile or arriving at the scene of law-violating behavior. What are those five options?

3. How does community-oriented policing help in dealing with juveniles?

4. One of the most important challenges the police face today is finding missing children. What is the AMBER alert program? What does it stand for? How did it get started and how does it work?

Multiple Choice:
1. Answer: c   2. Answer: d   3. Answer: c   4. Answer: e   5. Answer: c
6. Answer: a   7. Answer: d   8. Answer: c   9. Answer: e   10. Answer: b
11. Answer: d   12. Answer: b   13. Answer: a   14. Answer: b   15. Answer: e
16. Answer: b   17. Answer: d   18. Answer: a   19. Answer: a   20. Answer: d
21. Answer: c   22. Answer: e   23. Answer: e   24. Answer: e   25. Answer: a
26. Answer: d

True/False:
1. False   2. True   3. False   4. True   5. False   6. True   7. True   8. True   9. True
10. False   11. True   12. False   13. False   14. False   15. False   16. True

Fill-in-the-blank:
1. arrest
2. citation
3. fingerprinting
4. gang unit
5. juvenile officer
6. Miranda v. Arizona
7. police discretion
8. pretrial identification practices
9. search and seizure
10. station adjustment

WEBSITES

www.fsu.edu/~crimdo/fagan.html

Read more about police interrogation at the FindLaw site.
http://caselaw.lp.findlaw.com/data/constitution/ammendment05/09.html

Learn more about community policing at the community policing consortium site.
www.communitypolicing.org

To get more information on the Police Athletic League in New York, visit this site.
www.palnyc.org

Read the OLLDP Juvenile Justice Bulletin, *Effective Intervention for Serious Juvenile Offenders*, at www.justicestudies.com/WebLibrary.

Read the NIJ-sponsored publication, *Children in an Adult World: Prosecuting Adolescents in Criminal and Juvenile Jurisdictions*, at www.justicestudies.com/WebLibrary.

CHAPTER 15: THE JUVENILE COURT

After reading this chapter you should be able to answer the following questions:

1. How did the juvenile court begin?

2. What pretrial procedures are involved in juvenile court proceedings?

3. How is a trial conducted in the juvenile court?

4. What are the various forms of sentencing?

5. What can be done to improve the juvenile court?

CHAPTER SUMMARY

The first juvenile court was founded in Cook County, Illinois (Chicago) in 1899. *Parens patriae* was the doctrine that provided the legal catalyst for its creation. The court was an expression of middle class values, which began as a movement to humanize the lives of adolescents. The *child-saving* movement believed that social progress depended on efficient law enforcement, strict supervision and regulation of illicit pleasures. Lower-class children became the children to be saved as they were engaged in behaviors that challenged the social good. The sociocultural conditions also contributed to founding of the court since many citizens were incensed by the treatment of children during the last thirty years of the nineteenth century. Disenchantment with urban dwellers and the tripling of Chicago populations between 1880 and 1890 helped to give rise to the child-saving philosophy.

A series of decisions by the U.S. Supreme Court in the 1960s and 1970s demonstrated the influence of the constitutionalists on juvenile justice. The five most important cases were: *Kent v. United States* (1966), *In re Gault* (1967), *In re Winship*, (1970), *McKeiver v. Pennsylvania* (1971), and *Breed v. Jones* (1975). The Court attempted to balance the juvenile system similar to the adult justice system, but as some point out the abuses of the juvenile court are *Kadi*-like in that decisions are handed down based on the merits of each case.

The trial stage of juvenile court is divided into the *adjudicatory hearing*, the disposition hearing, and various judicial alternatives. Most states allow juveniles the right to appeal by statute, however juveniles do not yet have a constitutional right to appeal. Transfer of juvenile cases into adult court occurs either through *judicial waiver* or *legislative waiver*. Judicial waiver is the most common and takes place after a judicial hearing on a juvenile's amenability to treatment. The numbers of juveniles who are waived to adult court are likely to increase in the future.

Determinate sentencing is a new form of sentencing in juvenile justice and is replacing indeterminate sentencing in some jurisdictions. Additionally, increasing numbers of juvenile courts are using *blended sentencing* forms.

LECTURE OUTLINE

Introduction
- *Roper v. Simmons*: The juvenile death penalty case.

I. The Changing Juvenile Court
- Delinquency in America: In Family Court child defendant's welfare takes priority.
- Juvenile courts throughout the nation were patterned after the Chicago court. Records were sealed. Hearings were not open to the public and children were separately detained from adults.
- The court was founded on the premise it should act as a social clinic to serve the best interests of the children and not treat children as criminals.

A. Changes in Legal Norms
- Constitutionalists were concerned that children have procedural rights was well as rights to shelter, protection, and guardianship. A series of Supreme Court decisions in the 60s and 70s demonstrated the influence of the constitutionalists.
- Kent v. United States (1966) was concerned with the matter of transfer. The court held that Kent was essentially a denial of counsel, and that youths charged with felonies have the right to a hearing and essentials of due process.
- In re Gault (1967) affirmed that a juvenile has the right to due process safeguards in proceedings in which a finding of delinquency can lead to institutional confinement. The decision established that a juvenile has the right to notice of charges, right to counsel, right to confrontation and cross-examination of witnesses, and privilege against self-incrimination.
- In re Winship (1970) held that juveniles are entitled to the legal standard of proof beyond a reasonable doubt and not the former preponderance of evidence standard.
- McKeiver v. Pennsylvania (1971) denied the right of juveniles to jury trials. The Court stated not all constitutional rights are to be given juveniles, jury trials will put an end to the informal nature of adjudication proceedings, jury trials are not necessary for every criminal process, jury trials will bring unnecessary delays, and there is nothing to prevent states from adopting jury trials.
- Breed v. Jones (1975) held that a juvenile is entitled to double jeopardy protection in that a juvenile court cannot adjudicate a case and then transfer the case to adult court for processing for the same offense.

III. Juvenile Court Actors
- Judges, referees, prosecutors, and defense attorneys are the main participants in the juvenile court process and their roles have changed significantly in recent years.

A. Judges
- Judges are responsible for; setting standards, ensuring juveniles receive constitutional rights, ensuring the system is working fairly and efficiently, making certain adequate attorneys represent juveniles, monitoring of cases and progress of the child, being an advocate within the community, and in some jurisdictions serve as administrator of probation departments.
- David Matza refers to the justice of some judges like *Kadi justice* meaning judges make decisions based on the merit of each case and without apparent regard to rules or norms.

B. Referees
- Many courts employ the services of referees. Known as a *commissioner* in Washington state and a *master* in Maryland. They may or may not be members of the bar, but their responsibility is to assist the judge in processing youths through the courts.

C. Prosecutors
- Considered as the petitioner, the prosecutor is expected to protect society and at the same time ensure the children are provided their basic constitutional rights. Prosecutors may have to interpret juvenile law and procedure and some critics charge they have come to dominate the juvenile court proceedings.

D. Defense Attorneys
- The number of juveniles represented by defense counsel has been growing since the 1960s. Barry C. Feld found that many of the juveniles put into placement outside the home did not have counsel.
- Public defenders often do a better job of representing youth than do private attorneys.
- Juveniles with counsel were more likely to receive an institutional disposition.

IV. The Pretrial Procedures

A. The Detention Hearing
- Usually held within forty-eight to seventy-two hours.
- In some states intake officers conduct detention hearings, rather than judges.
- Juveniles may be assigned to four placement options: (1) detention home, (2) shelter care, (3) jail or police lockup, and (4) in-home detention.
- Schall v. Martin (1984) case may encourage the use of *preventative detention* of juveniles and some suggest it is intended solely for punitive punishment only.

B. The Intake Process
- Preliminary screening process to determine whether a court should take action and what type of action would be appropriate for the particular situation. Typically performed by probation officers.
- Intake units have up to five options; (1) dismissal, (2) *informal adjustment* or warning with requirement of restitution, (3) informal probation or casual supervision,

(4) *consent decree* or formal agreement between child and court without a formal finding, and (5) filing of a juvenile petition.

C. The Transfer Procedure
- Every state has some provision for transferring juvenile offenders to adult courts.
- *Judicial waiver*, the most common, takes place after a judicial hearing on a juvenile's amenability to treatment and contains procedural safeguards. Criteria typically used include age/maturity of child, seriousness of offense, past record, and relationship of the offender with parents, school and community.
- *Legislative waiver* is accomplished in five ways; (1) laws excluding certain offenses from juvenile jurisdiction, (2) lowering the jurisdictional age, (3) specifying age to specific offenses, (4) laws regulating specific offenses, and (5) concurrent jurisdiction.
- Legislative waivers are criticized as being inconsistent with rehabilitative philosophy.
- More and more juveniles are being transferred to adult court, however they are not necessarily the most serious or intractable cases.
- Juveniles who have previously been waived are likely to be waived again in the future.
- Studies conflict on the merits of transferring cases, some suggest transferring does not indicate more severe penalties, while others contend juveniles transferred to adult court receive longer sentences than their adult counterparts (by 2 years and 5 months).
- Reverse waiver and blended sentencing

V. The Juvenile Trial

A. The Adjudicatory Hearing
- Fact finding stage usually includes: the child's plea, presentation of evidence, cross examination of witnesses, and the judge's findings. Ten states allow jury trials, but they are seldom requested.
- The prosecutor has become the dominant force at these proceedings.

B. The Disposition Hearing
- Present trend is bifurcate the adjudicatory hearing into a separate dispositional hearing to allow probation officers to prepare a social history report for sentencing.
- Factors of school attendance and performance, family structure, degree of maturity, attitude, and sense of responsibility are all considered in determining a remedy for the adjudicated offense.
- In 1999, 24 percent of adjudicated youth were court ordered to out-of-home placement.
- The seriousness of the act has the greatest impact on judicial judgments.
- Informal factors of social and racial background of the youth and demeanor in the courtroom also affect a judges handling of juvenile delinquents.

C. Judicial Alternatives
- Depending on the size of the court, most alternatives consist of: dismissal, restitution, psychiatric therapy, probation, foster home placements, day treatment programs,

community-based residential programs, institutionalization in mental hospitals, county or city institutions, state or private training schools, and adult facilities.

D. The Right to Appeal
- Juveniles do not have a constitutional right to appeal, however most states grant them the right to appeal by statute.

VI. Juvenile Sentencing Structures
- Determinate sentencing is a new form of sentencing in juvenile justice, replacing the former indeterminate form.
- Blended sentences are increasing in which juvenile and adult sentences are imposed in combination to hold juvenile accountable for their actions.
- The Juvenile Justice Standards Project developed guidelines to base sentences on the seriousness of the crime rather than on the needs of the youth. The belief was that disparity in juvenile sentencing must end and attempts were made to limit the discretion of judges.
- Judges perceive the standards as attacking the underlying philosophy of the juvenile court.
- The get-tough changes are exemplified in both New York and Texas reforms.
- In 1995, Texas enacted legislation that a fourteen-year-old could receive the death penalty.

VII. The Death Penalty and Juveniles
- The United States has executed about 366 juveniles since the seventeenth century.
- The first case was for sodomizing a horse and cow.
- Georgia leads all states with 41 executions, followed by North Carolina and Ohio with 19.
- Twenty-five of thirty-eight states allow capital punishment for those under the age of eighteen when they committed their crimes.
- The cases of Stanford v. Kentucky and Wilkins v. Missouri in 1989 upheld the constitutionality of using the death penalty for juveniles.
- As of 2004 seventy-two individuals were on death row for crimes committed as juveniles with Texas holding the most.

KEY TERMS

adjudicatory hearing   The juvenile trial stage that typically consists of the child's plea, presentation of prosecutorial and defense evidence, cross-examination of witnesses, and the finding of the judge.

bail   The secured monetary sum an offender(s) uses to gain release from pretrial detention.

bifurcated hearing   Present trend of the juvenile court in which the adjudication and disposition hearings are separated.

child-savers   A movement of middle-class women at the turn of the twentieth century to rescue children from the filth, corruption and urban disenchantment caused by immigration.

consent decree   Formal agreement between the court and the juvenile in which the child is placed under supervision without a formal finding of delinquency.

constitutionalists   Justice reform movement, which maintains that children within the juvenile system deserve the same constitutional rights as adults.

detention hearing   The hearing in which an intake officer decides whether a juvenile should be detained in detention or released to their parents.

determinate sentencing   A form of sentencing that provides fixed sentences for offenses. The terms of the sentences are generally set by legislatures.

indeterminate sentencing   Sentencing in which a judge has wide discretion to commit a juvenile to the department of corrections or youth authority until correctional staff make a decision to release the juvenile.

informal adjustment   An agreement between a juvenile and the court that allows restitution to be made without a formal petition being filed.

informal probation   Youth aggress to supervised probation conditions without being formally adjudicated by the court.

intake   The first stage of the juvenile court proceedings in which the decision is made to divert the youth to alternative treatment or to file a juvenile petition.

judicial waiver   Occurs after a judicial hearing on the amenability of treatment for the juvenile offender and is the most common form of juvenile to adult court transfer.

jury trial   Regulated by state statutes and not permitted by constitutional rights for juveniles.

kadi justice   David Matza's description of juvenile court judges that act on the merits of each case and without regard to rules and norms, much like a Moslem market-place judge.

legislative waiver   Juvenile to adult court transfer that is determined by prescribed factors established through legislative acts, such as type of offense and age specific offenses.

referee   Juvenile court assistants that help judges process cases through the court. They may or may not be members of the bar and are known as both commissioners and masters in some states.

reverse waiver   In some states youths who are over the maximum age of jurisdiction may be sent back to the juvenile court if the adult court believes the case is more appropriate for juvenile court jurisdiction.

shelter care Facilities used primarily for short-term holding of juvenile status offenders or neglected children.

transfer The movement of a juvenile case into adult court for disposition.

Practice Test

Multiple Choice:

1. The vignette at the beginning of the chapter involved _____.
a. a crime committed against a police officer
b. O. J. Simpson
c. President George Bush Sr.
d. the issue of capital punishment
e. the death of Michael Jordan's father

2. The case of *Roper v. Simmons* ruled that _____.
a. juvenile have a right to an attorney
b. juveniles have a right to talk to their parents before questioning
c. juveniles have a right not to be searched at school
d. juveniles have a right to remain silent
e. it is unconstitutional to execute a person for committing a capital crime as a juvenile

3. In the *Roper v. Simmons* case, Christopher Simmons committed the crime of _____.
a. murder
b. rape
c. selling drugs to juveniles
d. arson
e. all of the above

4. What is the position of Barry Fled concerning the juvenile court?
a. he feels the juvenile court should be greatly expanded with more assest and options
b. he feels that the juvenile court should be allowed to handle serious felonies
c. he feels that juvenile courts should be abolished
d. he feels that juvenile courts should be restricted to people under 16

5. At the end of a juvenile trial the Judge issues a _____.
a. sentence
b. decision
c. disposition
d. guilty verdict
e. all of the above could be issued

6. The juvenile court trial is not called a trial but a _____.
a. disposition
b. fact finding
c. counseling session
d. mediation
e. juvenile trial

7. A group of people who believe that the justice reform movement, should maintain the idea that children within the juvenile system deserve the same constitutional rights as adults are called _____.
a. the child savers
b. the "Protectors"
c. the Mothers for Children
d. constitutionalists
e. Founding Fathers

8. What was the first Supreme Court case to deal with juveniles?
a. *In re Gault*
b. *Kent v. United States*
c. *In re Winship*
d. *McKeiver V. Pensylavania*
e. *Breed v. Jones*

9. Which case dealt with the issue of transfer to adult court?
a. *In re Gault*
b. *Kent v. United States*
c. *In re Winship*
d. *McKeiver V. Pensylavania*
e. *Breed v. Jones*

10. Gerald Gault received a sentence to a juvenile institution for the crime of _____.
a. buying drugs
b. selling drugs
c. sexual assault of a minor
d. murder
e. making lewd and indecent remarks on the phone

11. Which of the following rights were not granted in *In re Gault*?
a. the right to remain silent
b. the right to notice of charges
c. the right to counsel
d. the right to a jury trial
e. the right to cross examine witnesses

12. Which case dealt with the issue of "preponderance of the evidence"?
a. *In re Gault*
b. *Kent v. United States*
c. *In re Winship*
d. *McKeiver V. Pensylavania*
e. *Breed v. Jones*

13. The case of _____ ruled that juveniles did not have a right to a jury trial.
a. *In re Gault*
b. *Kent v. United States*
c. *Breed v. Jones*
d. *McKeiver V. Pensylavania*
e. *In re Winship*

14. The issue of double jeopardy was taken up in the case of _____.
a. *In re Gault*
b. *Kent v. United States*
c. *Breed v. Jones*
d. *McKeiver V. Pensylavania*
e. *In re Winship*

15. If a juvenile was tried in both an adult court and a juvenile court that would be called
_____.
a. innovative
b. a change of venue
c. a motion for discovery
d. double jeopardy
e. a preponderance of the evidence

16. What case granted juveniles the right against self-incrimination?
a. *In re Gault*
b. *Kent v. United States*
c. *In re Winship*
d. *McKeiver V. Pensylavania*
e. *Breed v. Jones*

17. Justice Abe Fortas said "There is evidence, in fact, that there may be grounds for concern that the child receives the worst of both worlds; that he gets neither the protection accorded to adults not the solicitous care and regenerative treatment postulated for children." In which case?
a. *In re Gault*
b. *Kent v. United States*
c. *In re Winship*
d. *McKeiver V. Pensylavania*
e. *Breed v. Jones*

18. Who does your authors consider to be the most important person in the juvenile court?
a. the judge
b. the probation officer
c. the prosecuting attorney
d. the defense attorney

19. Juvenile court assistants that help judges process cases through the court are called _____. They may or may not be members of the bar and are known as both commissioners and masters in some states.
a. assistants prosecutors
b. assistant judges
c. counselors
d. arbitrators
e. referees

20. In a juvenile court the prosecutor may be called the _____.
a. master
b. referee
c. petitioner
d. commissioner
e. social counselor

21. The movement of a juvenile case into adult court for disposition is called a _____.
a. transfer
b. upgrade
c. relocation
d. reassignment
e. hand over

22. What model of juvenile justice does Australia follow?
a. the rehabilitation model
b. the welfare model
c. the social model
d. the punishment model
e. the justice model

23. Which government has basically abolished the concept of *parens patriae*?
a. the United States
b. California
c. Mexico
d. Canada
e. Japan

24. The hearing in which an intake officer decides whether a juvenile should be detained in detention or released to their parents is called a _____.
a. a trial
b. a finding
c. a detention hearing
d. an analysis
e. a preliminary investigation

25. The constitutionally of preventive detention was confirmed by _____.
a. *In re Gault*
b. *Kent v. United States*
c. *In re Winship*
d. *McKeiver V. Pensylavania*
e. *Schall v. Martin*

26. A formal agreement between the court and the juvenile in which the child is placed under supervision without a formal finding of delinquency is called _____.
a. an agreement
b. a consent degree
c. an admission of guilt
d. a negotiation
e. a disposition

27. A juvenile to adult court transfer that is determined by prescribed factors established through legislative acts, such as type of offense and age specific offenses is called a _____
a. legislative waiver
b. political waiver
c. judicial waiver
d. prosecution waiver

28. When a juvenile court judge imposes both an adult and a juvenile sentence concurrently it is called _____.
a. unconstitutional
b. excessive
c. a blended sentence
d. an extended sentence
e. a follow-up sentence

29. The fact finding stage of the juvenile court proceedings is called a _____.
a. trial
b. disposition
c. adjudicatory hearing
d. probation hearing
e. evaluation

30. How many state provide for a jury trial for juveniles?
a. 2
b. 4
c. 6
d 10
e. Jury trials are unconstitutional for juveniles, the answer is zero

True/False:

1. Juveniles can be executed for capital offenses in America.

2. Christopher Simmons was tried for the crime of rape of a child under ten.

3. In the State of Florida, where Jeb Bush is Governor, a child of 6 can be tried for murder.

4. There is growing evidence that kids who are sentenced as adults come out worse than they would have if they are sentenced as juveniles.

5. Juveniles are not required to have a hearing before their case is transfer to adult court.

6. Since the case of *Fang v. New York* juveniles no longer have the right to remain silent.

7. Gerald Gault received a sentence to a juvenile institution for the crime of selling drugs.

8. The right to notice of charges for juveniles was granted by the case of *In re Gault*.

9. The case of *In re Gault* ruled that juveniles have a right to a transcript of the proceedings and the right of appellate review.

10. In *Winship*, the Court decided that juveniles are not entitled to proof beyond a reasonable doubt.

11. In a court of law, juveniles have all the rights that adults have.

12. A juvenile cannot be trial in both an adult court and a juvenile court. The Court has ruled that is double jeopardy.

13. To be a referee in a court you must be a member of the bar.

Fill-in-the-blank:

1. The court process wherein a judge determines if the juvenile appearing before the court committed the act with which he or she is charged is known as _____.

2. A criminal court, also called a(n) _____ that hears adult or juvenile cases. Juveniles may be waived (transferred) to this court system if they are accused of committing a serious offense.

3. The review of a juvenile court proceedings by a higher court is known as a(n) _____.

4. The review of the decision of a juvenile court proceeding by a higher court is referred to as a(n) _____.

5. An innovative form of detention facility, found in several locations across the nation, that is characterized by an open setting is a(n) _____.

6. The money or property pledged to the court or actually deposited with the court to effect the release of a person from legal custody is referred to as _____.

7. A legal standard of _____ establishes the degree of proof needed for a juvenile to be adjudicated a delinquent by the juvenile court during the adjudicatory stage of the court's proceedings.

8. Split adjudication and disposition hearings, also known as _____, are the present trend of juvenile courts.

9. The process of transferring (certifying) juveniles to adult criminal court is referred to as _____.

10. A 1975 double jeopardy case, _____ in which the U.S. Supreme Court ruled that a juvenile court cannot adjudicate a case and then transfer it over to the criminal court for adult processing of the same offense.

11. A charge, or _____ is made to an intake officer of the juvenile court that an offense has been committed.

12. A formal agreement between a juvenile and the court in which the juvenile is placed under the court's supervision without a formal finding of delinquency is known as a _____.

13. The name given to a group of twentieth-century reformers, _____, who advocated that juveniles deserve due process protections when they appear before the juvenile court.

14. A facility, a juvenile detention hall, that provides custodial care for juveniles during juvenile court proceedings. These facilities were established at the end of the nineteenth century as an alternative to jails for juveniles and are also described as a _____.

15. A _____, is conducted by an intake officer of the juvenile court, during which the decision is made as to whether a juvenile will be released to his parents or guardians or be detained in a detention facility.

16. A model of sentencing that provides fixed terms of sentences for criminal offenses is known as _____.

17. A constitutional prohibition against a second trial for the same offense. The Breed v. Jones decision (1975) ruled that juveniles cannot be tried in juvenile court and then be referred to the adult court, as that would constitute_____.

18. A criminal offense, punishable by death or by incarceration in a state or federal correctional institution, usually for one year or more is called a _____.

19. A form of detention that is used in some jurisdictions in which an adjudicated juvenile remains at home under house arrest, is also known as _____.

20. In juvenile justice, a sentencing model that encourages rehabilitation through the use of general and relatively unspecific sentences in which a judge has wide discretion is called an (a) _____.

21. An attempt to handle a youthful offender outside the formal structures of the juvenile justice system is called a(n) _____.

22. An arrangement, also known as a(n) _____, in which a delinquent is placed on probation instead of being adjudicated; where he or she is informally assigned to the supervision of a probation officer.

23. The 1967 U.S. Supreme Court decision that brought due process and constitutional procedures into juvenile courts is the _____ case.

24. A 1970 decision in which the U.S. Supreme Court decided that juveniles are entitled to proof beyond a reasonable doubt during adjudication proceedings is the _____ case.

25. The first stage, or the _____ of juvenile court proceedings, in which the decision is made whether to divert the juvenile being referred or to file a formal petition in juvenile court.

26 A police lockup or county holding facility for adult offenders is called a _____.

27. The process, also known as *certifying* or *binding over to the adult court,* of relinquishing a juvenile case to adult criminal court is known as _____.

28. A court proceeding in which a panel of the defendant's peers evaluate evidence and render a verdict is a _____.

29. A project jointly sponsored by the Institute of Judicial Administration and the American Bar Association that proposes juveniles' sentences be based on the seriousness of the offense committed rather than the "needs" of the child is called the _____.

30. A judicial approach similar to that of a Muslim judge who sits in the marketplace and makes decisions without any apparent reference to established or traditional rules and norms is known as _____.

31. The 1966 case of _____, is the first U.S. Supreme Court decision dealing with a juvenile court judgment on the matter of transfer.

32. A _____ is a legislative action that narrows juvenile court jurisdiction, but excludes from juvenile courts those youths charged with certain offenses.

33. The requirement that individuals who commit certain offenses be sentenced to a specified length of confinement if found guilty is a _____.

34. A 1971 U.S. Supreme Court decision that denied juveniles the right to a trial by jury is the case of_____.

35. A court process in which the defense counsel and the prosecution agree that the defendant will plead guilty, usually in exchange for a reduction of charges or a lessened sentence is known as _____.

36. The representative of the state in court proceedings: also called a county's attorney, state's attorney, district attorney , or _____.

37. A juvenile justice worker, who may or may not be a member of the bar, who assists judges in processing youths through the juvenile system is known as a _____.

38. Facilities that are used primarily to provide short-term care for status offenders and for dependent or neglected children are called _____.

39. The process, or _____, of certifying a youth over to adult criminal court which takes place by judicial or legislative waiver.

40. The imposition of juvenile and/or adult correctional sanctions on serious and violent offenders who have been adjudicated in juvenile court or convicted in criminal court is called _____.

41. Provisions that permit a juvenile who is being prosecuted as an adult in criminal court to petition and have the case transferred to juvenile court for adjudication or disposition is known as a _____.

42. Any court that has jurisdiction over matters involving juveniles can be called a _____.

Essay:

1. Today , three different positions have emerged concerning the role of the juvenile court. What are those three different positions? Explain each.

2. What was the case of *Kent v. United States* about and how was it decided?

3. What was the rights granted to juveniles in the case of *In re Gault*?

4. Explain, in detail, the famous case of *In re Gault*.

5. What are the 8 role responsibilities of the juvenile court judge?

6. What are the three roles of a defense counsel in a juvenile court?

7. The intake unit, especially in larger urban courts may have up to five options for the disposal of cases. List and explain those five options.

8. What are the five methods to accomplish a legislative waiver?

Answers Practice Test

Multiple Choice:
1. Answer: d 2. Answer: e 3. Answer: a 4. Answer: c 5. Answer: c
6. Answer: b 7. Answer: d 8. Answer: b 9. Answer: b 10. Answer: e
11. Answer: d 12. Answer: c 13. Answer: d 14. Answer: c 15. Answer: d
16. Answer: a 17. Answer: b 18. Answer: a 19. Answer: e 20. Answer: c
21. Answer: a 22. Answer: e 23. Answer: d 24. Answer: c 25. Answer: e
26. Answer: b 27. Answer: a 28. Answer: c 29. Answer: c 30. Answer: d

True/False:
1. False 2. False 3. True 4. True 5. False 6. False 7. False 8. True 9. False
10. False 11. False 12. True 13. False

Fill-in-the-blank:
1. adjudication
2. adult court
3. appeal
4. appellate review
5. attention home
6. bail
7. beyond a reasonable doubt
8. bifurcated hearings
9. binding over
10. Breed v. Jones
11. complaint
12. consent decree
13. constitutionalists
14. detention center
15. detention hearing
16. determinate sentencing
17. double jeopardy
18. felony
19. home detention
20. indeterminate sentencing
21. informal adjustment
22. informal probation
23. In re Gault
24. In re Winship
25. intake
26. jail
27. judicial waiver
28. jury trial
29. Juvenile Justice Standards Project
30. kadi justice
31. Kent v. United States
32. legislative waiver
33. mandatory sentencing
34. McKeiver v. Pennsylvania
35. plea bargaining
36. prosecutor

37. referee
38. shelter care
39. transfer
40. blend sentencing
41. reverse waiver
42. juvenile court

WEBSITES

Visit the OJJDP PowerPoint presentation " Juvenile Offenders in Court" at
www.justicestudies.com/WebPlaces

Learn about the Juvenile Detention Alternatives Initiative from the Annie E. Casey Foundation via
www.justicestudies.com/WebPlaces

Visit the National Institute of Mental Health's Child and Adolescent Mental Health Center's Web Site via
www.justicestudies.com/WebPlaces

www.juvenilenet.org

www.sgc.wa.gov/JUVSTD.htm

CHAPTER 16: JUVENILE CORRECTIONS

LEARNING OBJECTIVES

After reading this chapter you should be able to answer the following questions:

1. What types of experience do juveniles have in various institutional placements?

2. Why do some juveniles benefit more from institutionalization than others? How effective are institutions at correcting juvenile crime?

3. What rights do juveniles have while confined?

4. What can be done to improve juvenile correctional institutions in the United States?

CHAPTER SUMMARY

Community-based corrections is comprised of *probation, residential* and *day treatment* programs, and *aftercare*. Development of community-based corrections was encouraged in large part at the turn of the twentieth century and again in the 1960s. Support for community-based programs dwindled in the 1970s due to the pressure from hardliners persuading the public as to the danger of youth crime. The get-tough approach remained in place into the 1990s, as the public became more concerned about the threat to public safety of gun carrying, drug-using, and gang involved juveniles.

Early training schools were established as a means to protect children from the harsh treatment of adult facilities. During the 1970s, deinstitutionalization of status offenders and the elimination of staff brutality were the main reform issues. Reception and diagnostic centers do a relatively good job of evaluating the problems of institutionalized juveniles, however the programs are frequently not implemented when youths are transferred to a training school or camp-like facilities. Some ranches and camp programs provide good staff support for offenders but opponents argue that most of these youths could function well in community-based programs. Boot camps offer a disciplined and regimented setting that is generally accompanied by little programming.

Community-based corrections responded to critics through innovative developments such as intensive probation and more accountable means of juvenile probation. The costs of community-based corrections are still less than institutionalization and the fact still remains that more delinquents are treated in the community than are adjudicated to training schools.

The early years of the twenty-first century should be a time of expansion for community-based corrections. The prohibitive expense of long-term institutions may likely mean increased use of alternatives to institutions. Reformers of the 1970s may not see the level of decarceration attained that was once hoped for but economics will in all likelihood reserve institutions only for the hard-core and violent juvenile offenders.

LECTURE OUTLINE

I. Introduction
- Governor Rell
- Is the system broken?

II. Probation
- Probation has several connotations in juvenile justice. Probation is a legal system, an alternative to institutionalization, a subsystem of the juvenile justice system, and it includes the activities, functions, and services of transactions with the juvenile court, the delinquent, and community.

A. The Operation of Probation Services
- *Intake, investigation, and supervision* are the basic functions of probation services.
- The intake officer is generally a probation officer that must decide what to do with a case and whether to detain the juvenile. Ordinarily the child is released to the parents.
- Investigation requires probation officers to prepare social history reports usually within thirty to sixty days. Officers review arrest records, psychiatric or psychological evaluations, and any information from social agencies.
- Supervision is divided into casework management, treatment, and surveillance. The length of time one spends on probation is normally until the sixteenth or eighteenth birthday.
- Casework is typically divided up in categories depending on the juvenile's needs.
- *Surveillance* is required to make sure probationers comply with conditions of probation and they do not break the law. This may include parent visitations. *Revocation of probation* underscored the importance of surveillance with probationers.

B. Risk Control and Crime Reduction
- Current emphasis in juvenile probation is on *risk control and crime reduction*.
- The Office of Juvenile Justice and Delinquency Prevention has spent more than $30 million promoting restitution throughout the nation.
- Goals include; holding juveniles accountable, providing reparations, treating and rehabilitating juveniles, and punishing juveniles.
- A 1991 survey indicated that most juveniles referred to juvenile programs are diverted from the juvenile justice system.
- Intensive supervision programs responded to the criticisms of the 1980s and 1990s that probation was too lenient of punishment. Widely used in adult corrections, they are praised for keeping high-risk offenders out of long-term confinement.
- Recent developments of *Integrated Social Control* (ISC) model of intensive supervision integrates components of social strain, control and social learning theories.

- *Electronic monitoring* (inspired by a comic strip) is used for house arrest sentences, whereby youths remain confined in their own homes. They may be allowed to leave for certain purposes such as religious services, school, or medical reasons.
- Two types of electronic monitors include continuously signaling and programmed contact devices.

C. The Community Volunteer
- Probation began with the using of *volunteers*. Today over two-thousand programs assist in juvenile operations.
- Volunteer programs assist in helping offenders adjust to community life by providing one-to-one support, child advocate with teachers, employers and police, serve as role models, and in general help youth develop realistic responses to the environment.
- Criticism of using volunteers include: they create more work than they return. They are unable to handle serious problems and sometimes cause harm to clients.
- Parents may resist volunteers as an untrained worker.

III. Residential and Day Treatment Programs
- Typically reserved for those having difficulty dealing with the looseness of probation supervision.
- *Day treatment* programs are attended in the morning or afternoons with the juvenile returning home at night.
- *Residential* programs are usually *group home* or *foster care* placements where the juvenile is taken away from the supervision of parents.

A. The Types of Residential and Day Treatment Programs
- *Group homes* or *halfway houses* provide alternatives to institutionalization. They serve as short-term placement and are known as halfway-in or halfway-out.
- A well-developed group home model is the teaching-family group model used in the *Achievement Place* in Lawrence, Kansas. Also the *Criswell House* in Florida.
- The *House of Umoja* in Philadelphia (Sister Fattah) works almost exclusively with gang delinquents.
- *Day treatment* programs are more economical because they do not provide living or sleeping quarters. They generally serve males. Some examples are *STAY* and *AMI* but with the decline of federal funding many day treatment programs have closed their doors.
- *Wilderness* programs seek to help gain self-reliance. *Outward Bound* first established in Colorado in 1962 is the most widely used. *VisionQuest* began in 1973 in Tucson.

IV. Types of Institutional Placements for Juveniles
- *Training schools, reception centers, ranches and forestry camps, and boot camps* are the main forms of juvenile correctional institutions.
- *Adult prisons* are increasingly being used for juvenile corrections in the late twentieth century.
- There are twice as many private juvenile facilities as there are public facilities, yet private facilities hold less than half of the confined offenders.

- Newest information on juveniles in custody is drawn from Census of Juveniles in Residential Placement *(CJRP)*.

A. Reception and Diagnostic Centers
- Centers determine the best *placement* and *treatment plan* for each adjudicated youth.
- Average length of stay is thirty-four days. Physical and dental exams are typically given at this time. Psychologists, social workers, and staff evaluate each youth.
- A *diagnostic report* is sent with the youth when transferred, however they are frequently ignored by the receiving facility.

B. Ranches and Forestry Camps
- *Minimum-security* and reserved for youths who have committed *minor offenses*.
- Most forestry camps are located in Florida (16) and New York (14).
- Residents normally do conservation work in state parks.
- Escapes are common due to the *nonsecure nature* of the facilities.
- Private ranches are widely used in California. The average length of stay is 6.5 months.
- Residents are generally more positive about placement in a forestry camp or ranch than institutional placement. However, those that cannot handle these settings will repeatedly run away until placed in institutional settings.
- *Hennepin County Home School* is an innovative *coeducational* facility. The *Alpha* and *Beta* programs are treatment oriented with the Beta program for less serious offenders.

C. Boot Camps
- Emphasize military discipline and regimented training for a period of 30 to 120 days.
- The intent is to *shock the delinquent* into not committing more crimes.
- Boot camps are generally reserved for mid-range offenders and those that have failed lesser sanctions, yet not hardened violent offenders or sex offenders.
- In 1999, ten states had implemented about 50 boot camps for 4,500 offenders.
- Evaluations of boot camps suggest they experience *considerable instability* and are unable to implement well-developed aftercare services.
- Some studies have suggested their *recidivism rates are higher* than traditional facilities.
- *Death cases* such as the dehydration of a 14-year-old girl in South Dakota and the death of a 14 year-old (Anthony Haynes) in Phoenix tarnishes the image of boot camps.
- Critics often charge that boot camps are *abusive* in nature and no long-term rehabilitation effects are found.

D. Public and Private Training Schools
- Some training schools resemble prisons, while others look like college campuses.
- They are used more today than in the 1970s and 1980s.
- Training schools are a very expensive way to treat delinquent youths.
- Gangs are becoming a serious problem in some training schools.
- Massachusetts and Vermont have no training schools.

- Security is higher for public facilities verses private facilities and both medical and dental services are very good.
- Educational programs are usually accredited by the state and range from GED to vocational and academic programming.
- *Treatment modalities* range from transactional analysis and guided group interaction to drug and alcohol treatments.
- Treatment for females is often neglected in lieu of programs for males.
- Recreational activities are popular with residents and religious services are provided, however they tend not to be very popular with residents.
- Punishments vary and the time spent in solitary confinement is less than a decade ago.
- The use of force and mechanical restraints in training schools has recently increased.
- Bartollas suggests there are relatively few differences between private and public placements in terms of their effectiveness in reducing delinquency. Private facilities tend to be more flexible.

E. Adult Prisons
- Life on the inside is extremely austere, crowded and dangerous.
- Juveniles are subject to sexual and physical assaults.
- In October of 2000, Indiana stopped sending juveniles into the general prison population.
- Thirteen states permit the transfer of juveniles to adult facilities.

V. Training School Life
- Many studies present a frightening picture of what juveniles experience in confinement.

A. Training Schools for Boys
- Most studies support that training schools are a society of the strong victimizing the weak.
- Sethard Fisher defined *victimization* as a predatory practice, and *patronage* as building protective relationships for more advantageous situations on the prestige ladder.
- Bartollas suggests that dominant youths exploit submissive ones.

B. Training Schools for Girls and Coeducational Institutions
- Early studies suggested varying degrees of lesbian alliances.
- Propper found that homosexuality and make-believe families was just a prevalent in coeducational facilities as single-sex institutions.
- Bartollas found that females adhered more strongly to inmate groups and peer relations than did males. Females felt more victimized and did not harass or manipulate staff as much as males.

VI. Rights of Confined Juveniles

A. The Courts
- Courts pay more attention to adult prisons than juvenile institutions.

- Several courts have held juveniles have the right to treatment. *Morales v. Thurman* (1973) is the most extensive order ever issued in which several standards were established.
- *CRIPA* (Civil Rights of Institutionalized Persons Act) gives the Department of Justice the power to enforce civil rights violations of institutionalized persons.
- A consent decree in Puerto Rico addressed life-threatening situations and issues such as juveniles having to drink from toilet bowls.
- Access to the courts.

VII. Juvenile Aftercare

- The average length of stay in institutional care for juveniles is 9.8 months. *Aftercare* seeks to make an optimal adjustment to community living upon release from institutional care.
- Cottage staff consider performance in school, recreation, attitude, peer relations, and personality conflicts when reviewing a juvenile for release.

A. The Administration and Operation of Aftercare Services

- *Aftercare* is the responsibility of the state in forty-four states.
- Recidivism rates are lower than for traditional training schools (30 percent v. 50 to 70 percent).
- *Interstate compacts* are used to place children out of state when no acceptable home placement is within his or her state.
- Probation officers frequently carry the load of aftercare along with their other duties.
- Problems include sending youths back to same communities and families to expose them to the same problems they encountered originally.

B. Risk Control and Crime Reduction

- The current emphasis in aftercare is short-term behavior control.
- Intensive aftercare programs are increasingly being used much like supervision models. *"Lifeskills 95"* in California is designed for high-risk offenders.
- Aftercare frequently emphasizes drug and alcohol urinalysis.
- Revocation of aftercare may result in the youth returning to training school.

KEY TERMS

boot camp   Regimented facility consisting of military style discipline and training for mid-range juvenile offenders. The goal is to shock the offender into not committing delinquent offenses.

community-based corrections   Corrections programs that include probation, residential and day treatment programs, and aftercare which are linked between community programs and their social environment.

day treatment programs   Court mandated community based programs that juveniles normally attend in the morning and afternoon, and return home in the evening.

foster home placements   The foster home provides a temporary setting for juveniles who must be removed from their natural homes.

forestry camp   Minimum security facility for juvenile committing minor offenses. Residents normally perform clean-up work in state parks and other conservation related duties.

group home model   A placement for youths who have been adjudicated by the court. Called halfway houses and attention homes and serve a group of about thirteen to twenty-five youths as an alternative to institutionalization.

interstate compact   Procedures for transferring a youth on probation or aftercare/parole from one state to another.

Outward Bound   A wilderness-type survival program that is popular in many states as an alternative to institutionalization.

ranch   Public and private juvenile correctional institution that is usually less secure than training schools. Escapes are common and they typically provide a more normalizing experience for minor offenders

reception and diagnostic center   Juveniles are frequently sent to these centers for diagnosis of individualized treatment plans before their placement into a training school.

remote location monitoring   A type of house arrest where the juvenile is observed by a remote control device that transmit a signal or information concerning the location of the probationer.

residential programs   Placements for juveniles who are having difficulty with the looseness of probation supervision. Consists mainly of group homes or foster care placements.

restitution   Reparations offenders pay to victims and/or community as part of their disposition for a delinquent or criminal act they committed.

revocation of aftercare   Occurs when a probationer/parolee fails to meet the conditions of his or her aftercare agreement or commits another delinquent or criminal offense, and may lead to their return to training school.

social history report   A written report of a juvenile's social background that probation officers prepare for a juvenile judge to assist the court in making a disposition of a youth who has been ruled delinquent.

surveillance   A method probation officers use to ensure that probationers are meeting the conditions of their probation. Typically involves parental visitations and underscores revocation of probation.

teaching-family group home model   A well-developed group home model with specialized treatment programs to treat the more severe delinquency problems. Currently used in twelve states with Achievement Place, Criswell House, and House of Umoja being the most well known.

training school A juvenile correctional facility for long-term placement of juvenile delinquents.

volunteer programs Probation officers use volunteers for assistance of casework and helping offenders adjust to community life. They often serve as child advocates with teachers, employers and police.

Practice Test

Multiple Choice:

1. The vignette at the beginning of the chapter involved _____.
a. Governor Rell from Connecticut
b. Former President Bill Clinton
c. Governor Velsack from Iowa
d. Senator Baruch Obama
e. Senator George Allen from Virginia

2. This system allows offenders to remain in the community under supervision and subject to certain conditions imposed by the court.
a. parole
b. weekend jail
c. work release
d. furlough
e. probation

3. The initial decision is made about what to do with the law-violating juvenile at _____.
a. school
b. his home
c. intake
d. the time the judge sentences the juvenile
e. the probation hearing

4. The intake officer is usually a _____.
a. volunteer parent
b. probation officer
c. parole officer
d. police officer
e. school official

5. The *Desktop Guide to Good Juvenile Probation Practice* is published by _____.
a. the National Center for Juvenile Justice
b. the FBI
c. George Knox of the National Gang Crime Research Center
d. National Probation Association
e. National Criminal Justice Center

6. When a probation officer does a complete background check on a youth ruled delinquent to aid the judge in making the correct disposition it is called a _____.
a. background check
b. personal inspection
c. information search
d. social history
e. juvenile investigation

7. Reparations offenders pay to victims and/or the community as part of their disposition for a delinquent or criminal act they committed are called _____.
a. fines
b. restitution
c. gifts
d. probation commitments
e. taxes

8. Since 1964 restitution programs have _____.
a. rose during the 70s but declined during the 80s
b. decreased a little since 1964
c. rose dramatically
d. decrease substantially
e. rose about 10 percent

9. Studies on intensive supervision in your text have demonstrated that _____.
a. it does not work
b. it works very well in most cases
c. it works very well in all cases
d. neither the possible effectiveness nor the possible ineffectiveness of these programs had been carefully examine

10. A sentence imposed by the court whereby youths are ordered to remain confined in their homes for the length of the sentence is best called _____.
a. home prison
b. house arrest
c. juvenile jail
d. foster home placement
e. shock probation

11. A sentence imposed by the courts whereby youths are ordered to remain confined in their own homes for the length of their sentence is called _____.
a. probation
b. parole
c. weekday jail
d. house arrest
e. home furlough

12. The idea of electronic monitoring was inspired by _____-.
a. the NASA space shuttle
b. a comic strip in which Spiderman was tracked by a transmitter affixed to his wrist
c. the movie Batman
d. the James Bond movies
e. the company Nextel

13. A device which uses a transmitter attached to the probationer that emits a continuous radio signal is called a _____.
a. continuous signaling device
b. programmed contact device
c. global position system
d. 24/7 security device
e. supermax security

14. A device which calls the juvenile probationer by phone at scheduled or random times and uses various technologies to determine the identity of the person is called _____.
a. continuous signaling device
b. the phone security device
c. global position system
d. 24/7 security device
e. programmed contact device

15. A device in which the juvenile probationer wears a transmitter that communicates signals to a satellite and back to a computer monitor, pinpointing the offender's whereabouts is called a

_____.
a. continuous signaling device
b. programmed contact device
c. global position system
d. 24/7 security device
e. supermax security

16. Court mandated community based programs that juveniles normally attend in the morning and afternoon, and return home in the evening are called _____.
a. day treatment programs
b. work release
c. community probation
d. community parole
e. residential treatment programs

17. When juveniles are taken away from the supervision of their parents and are assigned twenty-four hours a day to their new placement in a group homes of foster care placement it is called a (an) _____
a. day treatment programs
b. work release
c. incarceration
d. community parole
e. residential treatment programs

18. What purpose does a group home provide?
a. provide an alternative to institutionalization
b. serve as a short-term community placement
c. serve as a "half-way in" setting for youths having difficulty adjusting to probation
d. all of the above

19. A placement for youths who have been adjudicated by the court which is sometimes called a halfway house or attention homes and serves a group of about thirteen to twenty-five youths as an alternative to institutionalization is called _____.
a. a jail
b. a group home model
c. a boot camp
d. a day treatment center
e. a home study program

20. The Associated Marine Institutes program is an example of a _____.
a. group home
b. nonresidential day treatment program
c. boot camp
d. small jail
e. intensive supervision program

21. What program uses the motto "Tell me, I'll forget. Show me, I may remember, Involve me, I'll be committed"?
a. The Juvenile Justice Department
b. The California Community Treatment Program
c. The Associated Marine Institutes
d. Project New Pride
e. The New York Division of Youth

22. To "overcome a seemingly impossible task" is one of the main goals of _____.
a. Teens Without Jobs
b. Mothers without Fathers
c. Outward Bound
d. The Police Athletic League
e. Juvenile Athletic Program

23. What is the name of the program that uses the idea of staff as parents, the use of rigorous outdoor activity, and the use of living history to connect youth to their heritage and culture?
a. Teens Without Jobs
b. VisionQuest
c. Outward Bound
d. The Police Athletic League
e. Juvenile Athletic Program

24. The program that juveniles are frequently sent to for diagnosis of individualized treatment plans before their placement into a training school is called a _____.
a. group home
b. halfway house
c. probation house
d. training center
e. reception and diagnostic center

25. Security institutions, such as ranches and forestry camps are _____.
a. usually reserved for the most dangerous delinquents who cannot be trusted to live in the city
b. usually reserved for repeat offenders to get them away from their friends and bad influences
c. usually reserved for offenders who have committed minor offenses
d. usually reserved for "white collar" offenses

26. A program that emphasizes military discipline, physical training, and regimented activity is called a _____.
a. boot camp
b. strict camp
c. halfway camp
d. deterrence camp
e. forestry camp

27. Experts have studied the California Youth Authority and concluded _____.
a. it is one of the most successful juvenile departments in America
b. it is new and innovative but not the best in the nation
c. the system fails in its most basic tasks because of antiquated facilities, violence and untrained employees
d. it has improved dramatically under the rule of Arnold

28. The avowed purpose of most training schools is _____.
a. the punishment of the juvenile
b. the deterrence of other juveniles
c. the completion of the juveniles education
d. the removal of the juvenile from society
e. the rehabilitation of juvenile delinquents

29. David Shichor and Clemens Bartollas's 1990 examination of the patterns of public and privates juvenile placements in one of the larger probation departments in southern California revealed that _____.
a. private juvenile placements were far more successful at preventing future crime
b. public juvenile placements were far more successful at preventing future crime
c. that there were relatively few differences between private and public placement
d. that church place were really the best schools for juveniles

30. The Federal Courts have mandated two major rights for juveniles in institutions, the right to
_____ and _____.
a. private rooms and clean water
b. a good education and private rooms
c. treatment and to be free from cruel and unusual punishment
d. appeal and good food
e. all of the above

True/False:

1. The maximum time a juvenile can spend on probation is three years.

2. Surveillance requires that the probation officer make certain that probationers comply with the conditions of probation and that they do not break the law.

3. Probation officer are part of the treatment of juveniles and therefore they have no law enforcement role.

4. When a juvenile is under house arrest, usually, they are not even allowed to leave the house to go to school.

5. The idea of electronic monitoring was inspired by the movie Batman.

6. In reality, there is no such thing as a remote controlled testing device for alcohol.

7. In fact, there are more than twice as many privately operated juvenile facilities as publicly operated one.

8. A program that emphasizes military discipline, physical training, and regimented activity is called a work farm.

9. Boot camps for juveniles include some type of work detail and allocate more than half the day to educational and counseling activities.

10. Studies of boot camps have found recidivism rates to be slightly higher or about the same as those of traditional juvenile facilities.

11. In the California juvenile prison system the prevalence of violence is common.

12. The youth gangs are not a serious problem in juvenile institutions.

Fill-in-the-blank:

1. A military-style facility used as an alternative to prison in order to deal with prison crowding and public demands for severe punishment is called a _____.

2. A correction program that links community programs with the social environment which includes probation, residential and day treatment programs, or parole is called

_____.

3. Court-required restitution in which a juvenile spends a certain number of hours working in a community project is called a _____.

4. An individual who donates his or her time to work with delinquents in the community is a

_____.

5. A guarantee provided by the Eighth Amendment to the U.S. Constitution against inhumane punishments is the right against is referred to as _____.

6. Court-mandated, community-based corrections program that juveniles attend in the morning and afternoon, then return home in the evening are the _____.

7. Correctional facilities, or _____, where residents usually do conservation work in state parks, including cleaning up, cutting grass and weeds, and general maintenance.

8. A home setting for juveniles who are lawfully removed form their birth parents' home is called _____.

9. A placement for youth who have been adjudicated by the court-called a *group residence, halfway house, or attention home*- that serves a group of about thirteen to twenty-five youths as an alternative to institutionalization: _____.

10. A form of community-based residential program that had some success with youthful offenders is a _____.

11. A residential setting for adjudicated delinquents, usually those who need a period of readjustment to the community following institutional confinement is called a

_____.

12. Procedures for transferring a youth on probation or aftercare/ parole from one state to another is a(n) _____.

13. A wilderness-type survival program that is popular in many states as an alternative to the institutionalization of juveniles is known as _____.

14. Training schools that operate under private auspices in which the country or state generally pays the school a per diem rate for the care of youths committed to these facilities, is known as

_____.

15. A court sentence under which the juvenile's freedom in the community is subject to the supervision of a probation officer is commonly called _____.

16. An officer of the court who is expected to provide social history investigations, maintain case files, supervise individuals who have been placed on probation, and to inform the court when persons on probation have violated the terms of their probation is known as a

_____.

17. Public and private juvenile correctional institutions that, like forestry camps, are usually less secure than training schools and have a more normalizing atmosphere are called

_____.

18. Facilities where juveniles who have been committed to correctional institutions frequently are first sent; these centers, commonly known as _____, diagnose youths' problems and develop individualized treatment plans.

19. The use of electronic equipment to verify an offender is at home or to track his or her whereabouts in the community, is referred to as electronic monitoring, but also as _____.

20. The social hierarchy that is established by residents in an institution is called _____.

21. Court-ordered repayment to the victim, often used together with community service as a condition of juvenile probation is known as _____.

22. The cancellation of parole and return of the offender to an institution; it takes effect if a juvenile on aftercare commits another offense or violates the conditions of parole and is called _____.

23. The entitlement of a juvenile who has been committed to a training school to receive any needed services like therapy or education, is called the _____.

24. A written report of a juvenile's social background that probation officers prepare for a juvenile judge to assist the court in making a disposition of a youth who has been ruled delinquent is known as a _____.

25. The observation of probationers by probation officers, intended to ensure that probationers comply with the conditions of probation and that they do not break the law is called _____.

26. A community-based residential program that has had some success with delinquent youth is known as a _____.

27. A correctional facility for long-term placement of female juvenile delinquents is called a _____.

28. The use of unpaid adult community members to assist probation officers in a variety of ways is known as _____.

29. The supervision of juveniles who are released from correctional institutions so they can make an optimal adjustment to community living is called _____.

Essay:

1. List all the people a probation might interview in a social history investigation of a adjudicated juvenile.

2. List ten common probation rules as presented in your text. (The text listed twenty).

3. To make the decision of whether to revoke probation, modify the conditions of probation, or place a juvenile outside the home, what questions should a probation officer consider?

4. List and explain each of the three broad types of restitution.

5. When it comes to making restitution and community service work, probation officers are key players, and in many jurisdictions it is up to a juvenile probation officer to do many things. What are those things as listed in your text.

6. How can community volunteers work effectively with juvenile offenders? What services can they provide?

7. What are some of the advantages of a nonresidential day treatment program?

Multiple Choice:
1. Answer: a   2. Answer: e   3. Answer: c   4. Answer: b   5. Answer: a
6. Answer: d   7. Answer: b   8. Answer: c   9. Answer: d   10. Answer: b
11. Answer: d   12. Answer: b   13. Answer: a   14. Answer: e   15. Answer: c
16. Answer: a   17. Answer: e   18. Answer: d   19. Answer: b   20. Answer: b
21. Answer: c   22. Answer: c   23. Answer: b   24. Answer: e   25. Answer: c
26. Answer: a   27. Answer: c   28. Answer: e   29. Answer: c   30. Answer: c

True/False:
1. False   2. True   3. False   4. False   5. False   6. False   7. True   8. False   9. True
10. True   11. True   12. False

Fill-in-the-blank:
1. boot camp
2. community-based corrections
3. community service project
4. community volunteer
5. cruel and unusual punishment
6. day treatment programs
7. forestry camps
8. foster care
9. group home
10. group home model
11. halfway house
12. interstate compact
13. Outward Bound
14. private juvenile placement
15. probation
16. probation officer
17. ranches
18. reception and diagnostic centers
19. remote location monitoring
20. residential social systems
21. restitution
22. revocation of aftercare
23. right to treatment
24. social history report
25. surveillance
26. teaching family group model
27. training school for girls
28. volunteer programs
29. juvenile aftercare

WEBSITES

Visit www.mycjspace.com , the Web site community for criminal justice professionals, students, and instructors. My CJ space allows you to create your own profile, communicate with others with similar interests, check out employment options in the justice field, and search the Web for criminal justice specific information and sites.

Learn move about John Augustus at the American Probation and Parole Association site. www.appa-net.org/the_early_years.htm

Learn more about the Outward bound program by visiting the Outward Bound Home page. www.outwardbound.org

Learn more about Glen Mills School at their home page. www.glenmillsschool.org/leftnar.html

www.iowacbc.org

http://virlib.ncjrs.org/corr.asp?category=44&subcategory=3

www.cjcj.org/

NOTES

NOTES

NOTES

NOTES

NOTES

NOTES

NOTES

NOTES

NOTES